The Believer's Hope

And Other Sermons

by

Oliver B. Greene

The Gospel Hour, Inc.
Box 2024
Greenville, S. C. 29602

First printing, June 1966 — 10,000 copies
Second printing, July 1967 — 10,000 copies
Third printing, January 1969 — 15,000 copies
Fourth printing, March 1970 — 15,000 copies
Fifth printing, November 1973 — 15,000 copies
Sixth printing, November 1974 — 15,000 copies

$4.00

CONTENTS

But God!

BUT GOD!

"BUT GOD raised Him from the dead" (Acts 13:30).

Two words in this verse are significant, powerful words. When we leave God out of our thinking and planning, we can rest assured that we will run into difficulty. Temptation will win the victory over us, sin will seduce us, self will sway us, and the world around us will warp and twist our thinking, our living, and our planning. We will daily be faced with seeming impossibilities, and these will irritate us until we in turn become irritable and unlovely.

Unbelief will undermine our faith and we will find ourselves slipping. Our stewardship for Christ will become a worry instead of a joy. When we leave God out of our daily living, fear creeps in; fear brings torment, and "he that feareth hath not been made perfect in love."

GOD IS LOVE — and when we look through eyes not focused on God, things wear a sombre hue, everything seems out of focus, and nothing is seen in proper perspective. But when our eye is singled on God, when we recognize Him as THE One who undertakes for us, THE One who is our life, in whom we live and move and have our being, then difficulties become opportunities — opportunities to trust Him, prove Him, and know Him.

The three Hebrew children knew an historical God the moment they moved into Babylon; but in the fiery furnace they discovered a *personal* God — they saw Him, they trusted Him, and He delivered them! When we recognize God in every phase of our living, temptations are overcome, sin has no attraction, and victory is ours. Self becomes ugly and loathsome — and we *deny* self. Unbelief is pushed aside; to serve God is a joy and delight, and our heart sings within us.

When we look through God's eyes and walk in the steps

7

of Jesus, all things are possible. We are His workmanship, created in Christ Jesus: and Christ is our life. In Him we live and move and have our being. When we are walking in the right spiritual position we are in the yoke with Jesus and He carries the burden. We have never seen Him with the physical eye; we have never touched Him with the hand of flesh; but when we touch God with a heart of faith and see Him with the single eye of trust, we rejoice with joy unspeakable and full of glory!

1. ". . . *Who can forgive sins BUT GOD only?*" (Mark 2:7).

It is true that only God CAN forgive sins. God so loved sinners that He give His only begotten Son, that whosoever believes in Jesus with all of his heart receives remission of sins, receives justification, is redeemed, and becomes a son of God:

"Behold, what manner of love the Father hath bestowed upon us, that we should be called the sons of God . . . Beloved, NOW are we the sons of God, and it doth not yet appear what we shall be: but we know that when He shall appear, we shall be like Him; for we shall see Him as He is!" (I John 3:1, 2).

But the skeptic asks, "If God is *Almighty* God, why would He be concerned about me and why would He forgive my sins?" The answer is in His Word: *God forgives our sins and saves us for the sake of the Son of His love:* "I write unto you, little children, because your sins are forgiven you for His name's sake" (I John 2:12). "And be ye kind one to another, tenderhearted, forgiving one another, even as God for Christ's sake hath forgiven you" (Eph. 4:32).

But how DOES God forgive our sins? What does God DO with our sins? Our sins were nailed to the cross of Jesus when He, the Son of God's love, willingly took our

8

place: "Who His own self bare our sins in His own body on the tree, that we, being dead to sins, should live unto righteousness: by whose stripes ye were healed" (I Pet. 2:24). "In whom we have redemption through His blood, the forgiveness of sins, according to the riches of His grace" (Eph. 1:7). "But if we walk in the light, as He is in the light, we have fellowship one with another, and the blood of Jesus Christ His Son cleanseth us from all sin" (I John 1:7).

It is true that we deserve hell; God could send each of us to hell and still be holy, pure, and just. Sinners *deserve* hell — but Jesus took our place. On Golgotha we see God at His best, giving heaven's best for earth's worst. God cannot die, but *He who died for our sins was God in flesh:* "To wit, that God was in Christ, reconciling the world unto Himself, not imputing their trespasses unto them; and hath committed unto us the word of reconciliation" (II Cor. 5:19). Only because of Calvary, only because of the blood of Jesus, only because of His willingness to take our place, can God forgive our sins. We deserve hell:

2. *"But GOD, who is rich in mercy, for His great love wherewith He loved us, even when we were dead in sins, hath quickened us together with Christ, (by grace ye are saved; And hath raised us up together, and made us sit together in heavenly places in Christ Jesus"* (Eph. 2:4-6).

God gives life. It is perfectly clear in the Word of God that we are dead in sins. All sinners are dead, spiritually: "And you hath He quickened, who were dead in trespasses and sins" (Eph. 2:1). "But she that liveth in pleasure is dead while she liveth" (I Tim. 5:6). Sinners, dead in trespasses and sins, walk according to the course of this world, they follow the prince of the power of the air, they are led by the spirit of the devil, they have their conversation in lust and sin. They fulfill the desires of the flesh and of the mind. Sinners are by nature the children of the devil.

ALL have sinned and come short of the glory of God; there is none righteous, no, not one. *All* we like sheep have gone astray. Sin gripped and bound us — until Jesus through His shed blood brought God's grace down to man. His grace quickened us by the Holy Spirit through the power of the Gospel, and now *we who believe* have life from Christ: "Verily, verily, I say unto you, He that heareth my word, and believeth on Him that sent me, hath everlasting life, and shall not come into condemnation; but is passed from death unto life. Verily, verily, I say unto you, the hour is coming, and now is, when the dead shall hear the voice of the Son of God: *and they that hear shall live*" (John 5:24, 25).

We have not only received life FROM Christ, we also have life IN Christ: "There is therefore now no condemnation to them which are in Christ Jesus, who walk not after the flesh, but after the Spirit. For the law of the Spirit of life in Christ Jesus hath made me free from the law of sin and death" (Rom. 8:1, 2).

Not only have we received life FROM Christ and have life IN Christ, but Christ IS our life: "When Christ, who is our life, shall appear, then shall ye also appear with Him in glory" (Col. 3:4). "I am crucified with Christ: nevertheless I live; yet not I, but Christ liveth in me: and the life which I now live in the flesh I live by the faith of the Son of God, who loved me, and gave Himself for me" (Gal. 2:20).

We deserve hell because we have sinned: BUT GOD, through His great love wherewith He loved us even when we were dead in sins, and through His rich mercy, allowed Jesus to die in our stead. Jesus who knew no sin was made sin for us that we in Him might be made the righteousness of God: "For He hath made Him to be sin for us, who knew

10

no sin; that we might be made the righteousness of God in Him" (Cor. 5:21).

3. *And the patriarchs, moved with envy, sold Joseph into Egypt: BUT GOD delivered him"* (Acts 7:9).

To the natural man, it would seem that for Joseph all hope was gone. His brothers seemed determined to destroy him. We may be persecuted, denied, pushed out and forgotten by man; sin may tempt us sorely, the world around us may be determined to damn us. The devil may torment us from every possible angle, our flesh may burn through lust and entice us to sin — BUT GOD is with us every second of every hour of every day, and He is able to deliver and protect His own: "There hath no temptation taken you but such as is common to man: BUT GOD is faithful, who will not suffer you to be tempted above that ye are able; but will with the temptation also make a way to escape, that ye may be able to bear it" (I Cor. 10:13).

When saints are obedient to God and when they fully trust Him, evil cannot overtake them. The hurricanes of hell cannot destroy them, the plagues of the demons cannot come nigh them. We are MORE than conquerors *through Him!* The time may come in the life of a believer when it seems that all hope is gone. It may seem that we are beaten, defeated — BUT GOD!

"What shall we then say to these things? If God be for us, who can be against us? He that spared not His own Son, but delivered Him up for us all, how shall He not with Him also freely give us all things? Who shall lay anything to the charge of God's elect? It is God that justifieth. Who is he that condemneth? It is Christ that died, yea rather, that is risen again, who is even at the right hand of God, who also maketh intercession for us. Who shall separate us from the love of Christ? Shall tribulation, or distress, or persecution, or famine, or nakedness, or peril, or sword?

11

As it is written, For thy sake we are killed all the day long; we are accounted as sheep for the slaughter. Nay, in all these things we are more than conquerors through Him that loved us. For I am persuaded, that neither death, nor life, nor angels, nor principalities, nor powers, nor things present, nor things to come, nor height, nor depth, nor any other creature, shall be able to separate us from the love of God, which is in Christ Jesus our Lord" (Rom. 8:31-39). Yes, it is God who keeps the saints!

4. *"And He said unto them, Ye are they which justify yourselves before men; BUT GOD knoweth your hearts: for that which is highly esteemed among men is abomination in the sight of God"* (Luke 16:15).

God knows the heart. Men may deceive themselves; it is possible for a person to trample upon his conscience until it is seared with a hot iron. It is altogether possible for men to make decisions and professions; they may talk a lot, they may wear a beautiful cloak of religion. Man looks on the outward appearance, but God looks upon the heart. The Pharisees were guilty of making the outside of the platter clean, but inside was filth — and God knew it, for God sees the innermost secrets of the heart.

Many times true believers are misunderstood by man, but God never misunderstands. Fellow-Christians do not always fully appreciate or understand us; sometimes they question our motives — but God knows the heart. God weighs the motive, and it is He who judges the heart. God sees the reality, and He estimates in pure holiness and righteousness. When we stand before the Judge who is righteous, we know that because He IS righteous He cannot judge wrong. He knows our hearts, and we know that we will receive from Him exactly what we have earned through righteous stewardship — through works directed in the right way and performed for the purpose of glorifying God.

It is altogether possible for us to deceive our neighbors, our loved ones, the pastor of our church, and even ourselves — BUT GOD cannot be deceived; He knows the heart! We should always bear in mind the fact that we will not be judged by man. We will not be judged by the minister in our community nor by our loved ones; but God Almighty will judge us in righteousness.

5. *"For our comely parts have no need: BUT GOD hath tempered the body together, having given more abundant honour to that part which lacked"* (I Cor. 12:24).

All true believers are one in Christ. In this great chapter from Paul's letter to the believers at Corinth, we are clearly taught that the body is ONE body with many members. We are all baptized into *one body* by the Spirit — whether we be Jews or Gentiles, bond or free, we have been all made to drink into one Spirit: *"For the body is not one member, but many."*

Paul then uses the human body to illustrate the true church. If the foot shall say to the hand, "Because I am NOT the hand, I am not of the body," does that make it true? If the whole body were an eye, could we hear? If the whole body were hearing, could we smell? "But now hath God set the members every one of them in the body, as it hath pleased Him" (I Cor. 12:18). God has a right to do just that. Since God purchased the church through the blood of Jesus, and since it is His glorious church, He has the sole right to place the members in the body as He desires.

Paul asked, "If they were all one member, where were the body?" There would BE no body. Therefore, "The eye cannot say unto the hand, I have no need of thee, nor again the head to the feet, I have no need of you. Nay, much more those members of the body, which seem to be more feeble, are necessary: and those members of the body, which we

13

think to be less honourable, upon these we bestow more abundant honour; and our uncomely parts have more abundant comeliness. For our comely parts have no need: BUT GOD hath tempered the body together, having given more abundant honour to that part which lacked: that there should be no schism in the body; but that the members should have the same care one for another" (I Cor. 12:21-25).

How glorious it would be if believers could realize that all born again people belong in the same body and that we should fellowship and work together for one purpose — to glorify the Lord Jesus by spreading the Gospel to every creature, winning souls through the preaching of the Word, building up the body by witnessing to those who need salvation.

God has given to each true believer his place in the body, and it is the duty of each member to keep in his own place and not covet the place of another. Envy and covetousness are ugly sins, but many believers are guilty of them.

Christ is the *foundation* of the church: "For other foundation can no man lay than that is laid, which is Jesus Christ" (I Cor. 3:11). Christ is the *head* of the church: "For the husband is the head of the wife, even as Christ is the head of the church: and He is the Saviour of the body" (Eph. 5:23). Since Jesus is the foundation and the head of the church, and we are members of His body, placed in a position that pleases God, then we should be pleased to please Him by serving in the capacity where He places us. Regardless of what we are, if we are what God wants us to be and if we are where He has placed us, then we are in a position to enjoy our spiritual birthright of abundant life, joy unspeakable and full of glory.

6. *"I have planted, Apollos watered; BUT GOD gave the increase"* (I Cor. 3:6).

14

God is the author, the giver, and the cause of all blessings. Writing to the Corinthians, Paul rebuked them for their carnality and childishness. He said, "I have fed you with milk, and not with meat: for hitherto ye were not able to bear it, neither yet now are ye able" (I Cor. 3:2). He reminded them that there was strife, envy, and divisions among them, and they were walking in carnality, acting like babies. Some were saying, "I am of Paul," some were saying, "I am of Apollos," and others said "I am of Cephas." Paul rebuked them by asking, "Who then is Paul, and who is Apollos, but ministers by whom ye believed, even as the Lord gave to every man? I have planted, Apollos watered; BUT GOD gave the increase."

It has pleased God to call, ordain, and send men to preach the Gospel. Some are given the grand and glorious privilege of sowing the seed, others water the seed — but *only God* can cause the seed to bring forth life and grow. When we who are believers are faithful in doing our part, God is always faithful in doing His part. If we faithfully sow the seed, faithfully water the planting, and in faith trust God to bring forth life through the Word, God WILL bring forth life. We must be born again, and the only way to be born again is through the incorruptible seed, the Word of God: "Being born again, not of corruptible seed, but of incorruptible, by the Word of God, which liveth and abideth forever" (I Pet. 1:23).

Ministers and personal workers should realize that God can get along without them. He could have provided some other way of salvation. He has a host of angels — He could have sent them to make disciples — but He did not. He has chosen through the foolishness of preaching to save souls. God could do *without* us but He is pleased to do WITH us if we will only allow Him to use us. He blesses our efforts, He answers our prayers, He honors our ministry; but all of our efforts, prayers, and services would be useless and vain without God's blessings. It is "not by might nor by power, but by my Spirit," saith the Lord of hosts. It is the Spirit that quickeneth; the flesh profiteth nothing.

Regardless of how long or how sincerely we preach and teach, if the blessings of God are not with us and upon us, our ministry is vain. If we faithfully sow the seed, if we faithfully water the seed sown by others, God will give the increase; but without HIM we can do nothing (John 15:5 b).

7. *"But as it is written, Eye hath not seen, nor ear heard, neither have entered into the heart of man, the things which God hath prepared for them that love Him. BUT GOD hath revealed them unto us by His Spirit: for the Spirit searcheth all things, yea, the deep things of God"* (I Cor. 2:9, 10).

God reveals truth. It was Paul who referred to Jesus as the author and the finisher of our faith (Heb. 12:2). Salvation is totally OF God, FROM God, BY God, THROUGH God, and without God there IS no salvation. God and Christ are one in salvation. Jesus said to His disciples, "Have faith in God" (Mark 11:22).

God is not found by searching; He is not found through wisdom; He is not found in a laboratory on a slide under a microscope nor in a test tube. The eye of man's perception cannot see the things of God. The ear of man's concentration cannot locate God. The brain of man, no matter how filled with wisdom, knowledge, and understanding, cannot figure out God with His love, mercy, and long-suffering toward man. The things of God are made known only through the Holy Spirit: "But the natural man receiveth not the things of the Spirit of God: for they are foolishness unto him; neither can he know them, because they are spiritually discerned" (I Cor. 2:14).

The natural man, regardless of how much education he

may have, cannot understand God, cannot appreciate God, and cannot receive God. The very desire to be saved is planted in the heart through the power of the Holy Ghost and hearing the Word of God:" So then faith cometh by hearing, and hearing by the Word of God" (Rom. 10:17).

"For ye see your calling, brethren, how that not many wise men after the flesh, not many mighty, not many noble, are called: BUT GOD hath chosen the foolish things of the world to confound the wise; and God hath chosen the weak things of the world to confound the things which are mighty; and base things of the world, and things which are despised, hath God chosen, yea, and things which are not, to bring to nought things that are: That no flesh should glory in His presence. But of Him are ye in Christ Jesus, who of God is made unto us wisdom, and righteousness, and sanctification, and redemption: That, according as it is written, He that glorieth, let him glory in the Lord" (I Cor. 1:26-31).

God gave up flesh in the Garden of Eden. Adam and Eve ate the forbidden fruit because Satan suggested that they would be as gods. And when their eyes were opened, they did not call on God their Creator for mercy, but immediately set about through their own thinking, planning, and ability to manufacture a covering for their nakedness. But God condemned the fig leaves, provided a blood sacrifice, and covered their naked bodies with the skins of innocent animals.

"But of Him are ye in Christ Jesus, WHO OF GOD is made unto us wisdom and righteousness, and sanctification, and redemption." God has made Jesus unto us wisdom — and apart from Jesus there is no wisdom. "The fear of the Lord is the *beginning* of knowledge" (Prov. 1:7). Christ

17

is our wisdom, He is our righteousness, our sanctification, our redemption — "AND YE ARE COMPLETE IN HIM" (Col. 2:10).

In the thirteenth chapter of John, Jesus told the disciples that He would go into Jerusalem, that He would be arrested, tried, convicted, and crucified. This broke their hearts. They had been walking and talking with Him for more than three years and it grieved them sorely to hear Him announce that He would be leaving them.

In John 14:1-6 He told them: "Let not your heart be troubled: Ye believe in God, believe also in me. In my Father's house are many mansions: if it were not so, I would have told you. I go to prepare a place for you. And if I go and prepare a place for you, I will come again, and receive you unto myself; that where I am, there ye may be also. And whither I go ye know, and the way ye know. Thomas saith unto Him, Lord, we know not whither thou goest; and how can we know the way? Jesus saith unto Him, I am the way, the truth, and the life: no man cometh unto the Father, but by me."

Thank God for Thomas! Perhaps he *did* doubt; he said, "Except I shall see in His hands the print of the nails, and put my finger into the print of the nails, and thrust my hand into His side, I will not believe!" (John 20:25). But it was also Thomas who said, "We do not know the way — show us!" Jesus replied, "I AM the Way, I AM the Truth, I AM the Life. *No man cometh to the Father but by me!*"

God reveals truth in Jesus — Jesus IS the truth. He said, "Ye shall know the truth, and the truth shall make you free" (John 8:32). God is the revealer of truth, and apart from God, the natural man cannot know truth. Truth sets free; but *truth originates in God.* Jesus was truth in flesh, and when we receive Him, we receive the fullness of God (Col. 2:9).

Sinners? Yes. *But God* forgives sins.

Dead? Yes. *But God* who is rich in mercy, has quickened us and raised us from the dead.

Persecuted, tried, tested, forgotten, ignored? Yes, *But God* was with Joseph, God was with Abraham, God was with the three Hebrew children, God was with Daniel — and God is no respecter of persons. He is the keeper of His saints.

Prone to sin, prone to be hypocritical, prone to profess and not possess? Yes. *But God* knows our hearts. He is able to deliver from hypocrisy and false profession; He is able to put within our bosom a new heart, a new spirit, a new life. If any man be in Christ Jesus, he is a new creation.

In the church we often feel neglected and unappreciated — *but God* has tempered the body together. God places us where we can best glorify Him — and if God is happy with us in the place where He has placed us, we should be happy to serve Him there.

We need blessings — yes. *But God* is able to bless our efforts, give the increase, take our feeble services and multiply them as He multiplied the lad's loaves and fishes.

Do we often read the Bible without fully understanding what we read? Do we hunger and thirst after righteousness? Yes. *But God* is the revealer of the deep spiritual things, He reveals these truths to us by His Spirit, and we cannot know them except as the Holy Spirit reveals them to us. When God is recognized as the One who undertakes for us, the One who loved us so much that He gave His

Son to die for us; when we realize that God is infinite, and that He is much more concerned about us than we could ever be concerned about ourselves, then all of our difficulties become opportunities to trust Him and all of our heartches become stepping stones to greater victories.

Dear reader, if you ever come to the place where you say to yourself, "What's the use? I think I shall just give up," remember:

"BUT GOD!!"

Who Can Be Saved?

WHO CAN BE SAVED?

"And when He was gone forth into the way, there came one running, and kneeled to Him, and asked Him, Good Master, what shall I do that I may inherit eternal life? And Jesus said unto him, Why callest thou me good? There is none good but one, that is, God. Thou knowest the commandments, Do not commit adultery, Do not kill, Do not steal, Do not bear false witness, Defraud not, Honour thy father and mother. And he answered and said unto Him, Master, all these have I observed from my youth. Then Jesus beholding him loved him, and said unto him, One thing thou lackest: go thy way, sell whatsoever thou hast, and give to the poor, and thou shalt have treasure in heaven: and come, take up the cross, and follow me. And he was sad at that saying, and went away grieved: for he had great possessions.

"And Jesus looked round about, and saith unto His disciples, How hardly shall they that have riches enter into the kingdom of God! And the disciples were astonished at His words. But Jesus answereth again, and saith unto them, Children, how hard is it for them that trust in riches to enter into the kingdom of God! It is easier for a camel to go through the eye of a needle, than for a rich man to enter into the kingdom of God.

"And they were astonished out of measure, saying among themselves, **Who then can be saved?** And Jesus looking upon them saith, With men it is impossible, but not with God: for with God all things are possible" (Mark 10:17-27).

The Word of God has always astounded men. After the interesting interview between the rich young ruler and the Lord Jesus, Jesus said to His disciples, "How hardly shall they that have riches enter into the kingdom of God." The disciples were astonished at His words; but Jesus said again, "How hard is it for them that trust in riches to enter into the kingdom of God." It is not **money** that damns, but putting **trust** (or faith) in riches.

Jesus then said, "It is easier for a camel to go through the eye of a needle than for a rich man to enter into the kingdom of God!" When Jesus said that, the disciples were —in everyday language—"flabbergasted." That statement "floored" them. The Scripture says, "They were astonished **out of measure.**" They then asked, "WHO THEN CAN BE SAVED?" The only place to find the answer to that question is in the Bible, because the Word of God is the only book on this earth that tells us about salvation, who **provided** salvation, and who can be saved.

Let us first look into the Old Testament. Isaiah is the "Gospel of John" of the Old Testament. The Gospel of John is the salvation book of the New Testament. Isaiah tells us more about the coming Saviour, the Lamb of God, than does any other Old Testament writer. I suppose the fifty-third chapter of Isaiah is loved by as many people as any other one chapter in all the Bible, with the possible exception of the twenty-third Psalm. In Isaiah 53:6 we read: "ALL we like sheep have gone astray; we have turned every one to his own way; and the Lord hath laid on Him the iniquity of us ALL."

Isaiah plainly tells us that we are all "in the same boat," spiritually speaking. We are all in the same spiritual category—"all we, like sheep, have gone astray." In the words of Paul, "There is none righteous, no, not one . . . there is none that seeketh after God" (Rom. 3:10, 11). All men are sinners by nature; they are born sinners; ALL have gone astray.

But thank God for the last half of Isaiah 53:6: Jehovah, the heavenly Father, the God of our Lord and Saviour Jesus Christ, has laid on Jesus the Lamb "the iniquity of us all." That one verse of Scripture tells us clearly and fully who can be saved — ALL! If Jehovah God laid on Jesus the

24

iniquity of us all, then we can say without reservation that every sin ever committed or ever **to be committed** was placed upon the Lamb of God, and He nailed those sins to His cross, paying for sin in full.

Just before Jesus literally passed His life back to the Father, He cried out, **"It is finished!"** (John 19:30). He paid the sin-debt. It is no longer the "sin-question," but the "Son-question." The answer you give to the question, "What think ye of Christ?" will determine where you spend eternity. If you believe in your heart that He is the virgin-born Son of God, that He died according to the Scriptures, was buried according to the Scriptures, and was raised according to the Scriptures (I Cor. 15:1-4), you will be in that number when the saints go marching in; but if you believe that Jesus was just "a good man . . . a great teacher . . . a great leader . . . the founder of a religion," you will burn in hell. "Believe on the Lord Jesus Christ, and thou shalt be saved . . ." (Acts 16:31). "That if thou shalt confess with thy mouth the Lord Jesus, and shalt believe in thine heart that God hath raised Him from the dead, thou shalt be saved" (Rom. 10:9).

To believe that Jesus is the Christ, the Son of God, settles the question of whether or not YOU can be saved. Whosoever will believe in his heart that Jesus is the Christ, the only begotten Son of God, "hath everlasting life."

Now let us turn to the New Testament: "For God so loved the world, that He gave His only begotten Son, that whosoever believeth in Him should not perish, but have everlasting life" (John 3:16). This verse is often referred to as "the Gospel in a nutshell." Certainly we need not call up any professor of religion and ask him what John 3:16 means, for the meaning is very clear. **God loved** . . . God **so** loved . . . God **so loved the world**—and beloved, that takes in everyone and excludes no one. If you are in the world, God loves you! God so loved the world that He gave

His only begotten Son. The only begotten of God was given for the world—for WHOSOEVER—and that excludes no one, but includes everyone. "That whosoever believeth"— please note: Not "Whosoever learneth ... liveth ... giveth ... or doeth," but "Whosoever BELIEVETH in Him should not perish, but have everlasting life!" All are included, not one is excluded. Who can be saved? **Anyone!** All who come to God by Jesus Christ.

The "salvation book" again proclaims, ". . . Him that cometh to me I will in no wise cast out" (John 6:37). According to the words of Jesus, "all ones" who come to Him, He will receive. Under no circumstances will He cast them out—IF they come to Him for salvation. Jesus did not say "If the **elect**, the **select**, or the **predestined** come," but **"Him that cometh to me."** When the Bible uses the masculine pronoun "him," it means mankind—male, female, rich, poor, wise, foolish, bond or free, regardless of color or creed. "Him"—**any** "him," **all** "hims" who come to Jesus, He saves. He casts out no one who comes to Him for salvation.

Peter adds a spiritual exclamation point to the fact that ALL can be saved: "The Lord is not slack concerning His promise, as some men count slackness; but is longsuffering to us-ward, not willing that any should perish, but that all should come to repentance" (II Pet. 3:9). What is "His promise"? Please note—it is singular, not plural. Personally, I believe that this Scripture refers to the promise of salvation. Someone has said there are 85,000 promises in the Bible for a believer and I do not doubt that. I have never counted them, but I do not doubt that there are that many glorious promises for the Christian; but this is **"promise"** (singular), and I believe the Spirit is here referring to the promise of salvation. The promise is to ALL—all who will come to God by Jesus Christ, all who labor and are heavy laden. All who come, He will in no wise cast out. "Come now, and let us reason together—come ALL!"

The Lord is longsuffering; He is not willing that any—not even one—should perish, but that all should come to repentance. The answer to the question, "Who then can be saved?" is clearly stated in these words: ". . . Not willing that ANY should perish, but that ALL should come to repentance!" So my dear friend, if you burn in hell at the end of life's journey, it will not be God's will; it will be because of your refusal to accept the finished work of the Lord Jesus—the gift of God, salvation by grace through faith, minus works (Eph. 2:8, 9). Never let anyone tell you that you are "elected" to be lost. God loves all, and it is not His will that any perish, but that all come to repentance and be saved!

Indeed I believe in the sovereignty of God. I believe in Bible election and in Bible predestination. I do not profess to **understand** the sovereignty of God, but I can understand John 3:16! I can understand John 3:36, John 5:24, and II Peter 3:9. I KNOW God loved the whole world, He gave Jesus to **die** for the whole world, and "whosoever will, let him drink of the water of life freely."

There is another passage I want us to see, and if this does not settle the salvation question in your mind, then dear friend, you have a **closed** mind; you are married to a religion, a preacher, a cult, and you are not willing to follow the Word of God.

Speaking to the Jews—His own people, the elect of the Old Testament era—Jesus said, "Search the Scriptures; for in them ye think ye have eternal life: and they are they which testify of me. AND YE WILL NOT COME TO ME, THAT YE MIGHT HAVE LIFE" (John 5:39, 40). ("They which testify of me" refers to the Old Testament Scriptures —Isaiah, Zechariah, Malachi, the Psalms. All through the Old Testament, beginning at Genesis 3:15 and going through Malachi, we see Jesus—the Lamb, the High Priest, the

Saviour, the King. Jesus is the center of the Old Testament Scriptures.)

The Jews were sticklers for the Law; they were students of the Word. They studied, read, and searched—but they were willingly ignorant, spiritually blinded by Judaism. They refused to see the Lamb in Isaiah 53. They refused to see the Saviour in Psalm 22 and 23. They closed eyes and mind to the truth, and the Truth is the only thing that will set men free: ". . . Ye shall know the truth, and the truth shall make you free" (John 8:32). The Jews searched the Scriptures, but refused to come to the Lord Jesus that they might have life! They were not lost, doomed, and damned because they were not "elected," because they were not "chosen," or because they were not "predestined." They were lost, they died in sin and opened their eyes in hell because "YE WILL NOT COME TO ME, THAT YE MIGHT HAVE LIFE." That settles it.

The sovereignty of God and the free will of man do not clash. They run through the Bible in parallel, like the rails on a railroad. They do not clash nor conflict. The sovereignty of God is a fundamental of the faith. The free will of man is just as truly a fundamental of the faith. Therefore, all who will come to God by Jesus Christ can be saved, regardless of who they are, regardless of nationality, regardless of educational, social, or monetary standing. Regardless of all else, let him that is thirsty come to the fountain of life, and drink freely.

"Come unto me, all ye that labour and are heavy laden, and I will give you rest" (Matt. 11:28). ". . . Him that cometh to me I will in no wise cast out" (John 6:37). "Come now, and let us reason together, saith the Lord: though your sins be as scarlet, they shall be as white as snow; though they be red like crimson, they shall be as wool. If ye be willing and obedient, ye shall eat of the good of the land: But if ye refuse and rebel, ye shall be devoured with

28

the sword: for the mouth of the Lord hath spoken it"
(Isaiah 1:18-20).

HOW ARE SINNERS SAVED?

Religions have done a good job of confusing people, but
you may rest assured that God is not the author of confusion, but of a sound mind. I Peter 2:6 tells us, ". . . He
that believeth on Him shall not be confused." If you are
confused, God is not responsible for it; the devil is the author
of confusion. Jesus is the author of life, truth, and of perfect, unshakeable assurance.

There is only one way to be saved. Every verse in the
New Testament that has to do with salvation is singular.
Jesus said, "I am the Bread of life; I am the Water of life;
I am the good Shepherd; I am the Door; I am the Way, the
Truth, and the Life. NO MAN COMETH UNTO THE
FATHER BUT BY ME."

There are many Scriptures which declare that the Door
to heaven is One, the Way to heaven is One. There are not
two ways, or more, to be saved; there is only ONE.

I know of no passage that is clearer than that in Acts 16.
Paul preached the simple Gospel to Lydia, and she was converted. He preached the same simple Gospel to a fortune-
teller, and **she** was converted. He preached the same Gospel
to a jailer, and **he** was converted. **What Gospel did he
preach?**

The jailer was at the point of taking his own life, thinking
his prisoners had all fled, when Paul cried out, "Do thyself
no harm: for we are all here!" The jailer called for a light,
sprang in where Paul and Silas were, and said, "SIRS,
WHAT MUST I DO TO BE SAVED?" That is the question
we are now about to answer. **What must a sinner do to become a Christian?** How **does** a sinner become a Christian?
Through what method, school, plan or trick does one become a Christian?

Beloved, it is not a plan, scheme, nor trick. The answer

is simple: "BELIEVE ON THE LORD JESUS CHRIST, AND THOU SHALT BE SAVED, AND THY HOUSE" (Acts. 16:31). Let me point out one little word: "ON." Paul and Silas did not say, "Do you believe there is a God?" ("The devils also believe, and tremble"—James 2:19). On every occasion when the demons met Jesus here on earth, they recognized and confessed Him to be God's Son, but the demons are not saved. An intellectual belief will not save you. Believing with the head is not salvation. Paul and Silas said, "Believe ON . . ." and to believe ON is to trust, to literally thrust yourself upon Jesus, fling yourself upon Him, and rest on Him. It is not how you feel, nor how you think, nor how you react—but **how you believe in your heart concerning Jesus Christ.**

If with your heart you believe that Jesus Christ was born of the virgin Mary, that God Almighty is His Father, that He lived a sinless life on earth, died on the cross according to the Scriptures, was buried and God raised Him according to the Scriptures, **you are saved!** Let me illustrate:

You can believe that an automobile is an automobile—but it will never take you anywhere until you trust yourself to get in it. You can believe that an airplane is an airplane—but it will never take you on a flight until you trust it enough to get on it. You can believe that a train is a train—but it will not take you across the country until you walk into a coach, sit down and trust the rails, the coach, the engineer and others who have to do with running the train. You can believe that a chair is a chair, but you will never know the comfort of resting in it until you sit down.

Dear sinner, you undoubtedly have faith in a train, a plane, an automobile, a bridge, a ship, or a chair; and if you will put the same faith in Jesus Christ that you put in those material things, entrust yourself to Him, trust your soul into His hands, place everything by faith into the hands of Jesus, He will save your soul!

30

Perhaps someone is saying, "I wonder if I have **enough** faith." Faith does not come by inches, ounces, or pints. If you have any faith at all, you have enough faith to be saved. Jesus said that if you have faith as a grain of mustard seed, you can remove mountains. It is not the quantity of faith, dear friend, **but in whom you place that faith.** "What think ye of Christ? Whose Son is He?" Confess Him with your mouth, believe on Him with your heart, and you will be saved (Romans 10:9, 10). It is not a question of **how much** faith you have, but **in whom** do you have your faith?

You may say, "Brother Greene, perhaps I do not have **the right kind** of faith." There is only ONE kind of faith. There are no different **brands** of faith, as of gasoline, toothpaste, or shoes. There is only one kind of faith. Take the faith you have in a chair when you sit on that chair, put that faith in Jesus Christ, and **He will save your soul.**

"For by grace are ye saved through faith; and that not of yourselves; it is the gift of God" (Eph. 2:8). Grace is God's part, faith is your part; but how do you get that faith?

"So then faith cometh by hearing, and hearing by the Word of God" (Rom. 10:17). The very faith through which you are made the recipient of God's grace is given to you by God when you hear His Word. Hear the Word, believe the Word, and God implants faith that will embrace salvation.

"SALVATION IS OF THE LORD" (Jonah 2:9b). It will be a happy day in the lives of some dear preachers and Christian workers when they realize and admit the Bible fact that man cannot save sinners, man cannot help God save sinners. All we can do is tell unbelievers what Jesus has done for them and explain to them that it is by simply trusting in His finished work that we are saved. Jesus paid it all—and paid in full. The sin-debt is not **being** paid, it is not **going to be** paid, it IS PAID in full.

31

"Who His own self bare our sins in His own body on the tree, that we, being dead to sins, should live unto righteousness: by whose stripes ye were healed" (I Peter 2:24). This marvelous bit of holy Scripture clearly declares that Jesus "BARE OUR SINS." He is not **going** to bear them. He will not **at some future date** bear them, He is not bearing them now—**He has already BORNE them.** It is in the past. When He said, "Father, it is finished," the sin-debt had been paid in full, and a debt that has been paid in full cannot be paid by another. Jesus Christ satisfied the heart and holiness of God, and in Christ we are complete (Col. 2:10).

If you are lost, the tragedy of your lost estate is this: Your sin-debt has been paid. Jesus bore your sins on His cross. He carried your sins to Calvary and nailed them to the tree. All you need do is believe that He did that, receive His finished work by faith—and He will save you. Salvation is a gift; the gift has already been purchased, and God presents it to you simply for the receiving. "As many as received Him, to them gave He power to become the sons of God, even to them that believe on His name: which were born . . . born of God" (John 1:12, 13).

Dear unbeliever, believe on the Lord Jesus Christ. By faith, place yourself on Him. By faith, fling yourself at His feet, look up to Him in prayer, and simply say, "Lord Jesus, I receive you as my Saviour!" He will save you—and you will know it.

WHY DOES GOD SAVE US?

Who can be saved? **ALL.**

How are we saved? **By grace through faith in the finished work of Jesus Christ.**

Now—Why did God love me so much that He gave Jesus to die on the cross, and literally turned His head while Jesus died? He heard the Son cry out, "My God, My God, why hast thou forsaken me?" But still God kept His head turned while Jesus bore our sins in His own body on the cross.

WHY? The answer is clearly stated in God's Word:

"And be ye kind one to another, tenderhearted, forgiving one another, EVEN AS GOD FOR CHRIST'S SAKE HATH FORGIVEN YOU" (Eph. 4:32).

While we were yet sinners, God loved us. While we were without strength—enemies to God—Jesus died for us. (Please read Romans 5:1-13.) Why such love? The answer: That God, for the sake of His Son, could be just—and still justify the ungodly who put their faith in the shed blood of Jesus Christ, "and hath raised us up together, and made us sit together in heavenly places in Christ Jesus, **that in the ages to come He might shew the exceeding riches of His grace in His kindness toward us through Christ Jesus**" (Eph. 2:6, 7).

The scriptural answer to the question, "Why does God save the sinner?" is simply this: God saves us for the sake of the Son of His love, His only begotten Son, that in the ages to come, in the eternity of eternities, God may display in the Pearly White City, **the Bride of Christ**—the Church without spot or wrinkle. God will display to all of His creatures and His creations, the unsearchable, unknowable, unnameable riches of His saving grace!

Salvation is **of** the Lord, **through** the Lord, **by** the Lord— and **for the glory of God's Christ.**

Eternal Life

ETERNAL LIFE

"For God so loved the world, that He gave His only begotten Son, that whosoever believeth in Him should not perish, but have everlasting life" (John 3:16).

Religion and ministers who are dedicated to their denomination, denominational terms and man-made doctrine have done a good job of confusing poor, lost sinners; but the Word of God is clear and understandable. "The entrance of thy words giveth light; it giveth understanding..." (Psalm 119:130).

In I John 1:4, 5 we read, "And these things write we unto you, that your joy may be full. This then is the message which we have heard of Him, and declare unto you, that God is light, and in Him is no darkness at all."

Dealing with spiritual matters must be done from the textbook of spiritual things — the Word of God. We cannot hope to understand the Word of God unless we compare Scripture with Scripture, spiritual things with spiritual. The best commentary on the Bible is THE BIBLE. In this study we will use only the Bible as our textbook, and "Thus saith the Lord" as the foundation for this message.

"These things have I written unto you that believe on the name of the Son of God that ye may know that ye have eternal life, and that ye may believe on the name of the Son of God" (I John 5:13).

Not one word in the Bible was put there to fill up space. Every verse has a definite place in declaring divine truth — and truth makes men free. This verse tells us that we may KNOW we have eternal life. There is absolutely no such thing as salvation apart from assurance. Any person who is genuinely born again is just as sure he is alive **spiritually** as he is sure he is alive **physically.** If you do not know you are saved as surely as you know you are breathing, then the devil has given you a counterfeit. (Satan is the master counterfeiter in spiritual things.) The assurance of eternal life is clearly and most completely set forth in the precious written Word of God.

The Scriptures positively indicate that assurance is entirely apart from **"feelings."** Nothing changes more rapidly and more often than our personal feelings. Feelings may change many times during the day — and even during the night. We do not know that we are saved by "feeling" saved; we know that we have eternal life through the written testimony of Almighty God. **"Ye shall know the truth, and the truth shall make you free ... If the Son therefore shall make you free, ye shall be free indeed"** (John 8:32, 36).

The true believer does not "hope" that he has eternal life, or "think" that he has eternal life. The truly born again person KNOWS he has eternal life, and he is assured that this gift of God is his NOW. When the unbeliever accepts the Lord Jesus Christ as Saviour, he embraces the Word of God and acknowledges that it IS God's Word, and **the Word** is his assurance of salvation.

To doubt the Word of God is to doubt God: "In the beginning was the Word, and the Word was with God, and the Word WAS God ... and the Word was made flesh, and dwelt among us, (and we beheld His glory, the glory as of the only begotten of the Father,) full of grace and truth" (John 1:1, 14).

Jesus said, "Verily, verily, I say unto you, Except ye eat the flesh of the Son of man, and drink His blood, ye have no life in you" (John 6:53). This means literally appropriating, assimilating, and receiving the Word of God into the heart. It is impossible for God to lie (Heb. 6:18 and Tit. 1:2). God's Word tells me, "In the beginning was the Word, and the Word was with God, and the Word was

God," ... and "As many as received Him, to them gave He power to become the sons of God, even to them that believe on His name: which were born ... born of God" (John 1:12, 13). To doubt those words is to doubt God — "and he that doubteth is damned..." (Rom. 14:23).

One who cannot trust Christ and believe God's Word, cannot be saved. We are saved by God's grace; and saving grace becomes ours by faith (Eph. 2:8, 9). Faith becomes ours by hearing, and hearing by the Word of God (Rom. 10:17). Therefore, one who cannot believe the Word cannot be saved.

HOW DO WE RECEIVE ETERNAL LIFE?

"And I give unto them eternal life; and they shall never perish, neither shall any man pluck them out of my hand" (John 10:28). The Lord Jesus Christ — and He alone — can give eternal life. He came into the world for the purpose of giving eternal life to all who would believe. He came "to seek and to save that which was lost" (Luke 19:10).

"The thief cometh not, but for to steal, and to kill, and to destroy: **I am come that they might have life, and that they might have it more abundantly"** (John 10:10). There is a vast difference between **everlasting existence** and **eternal life.** Man will never cease to be: **The sinner will exist throughout eternity,** and his death will be everlasting! But Jesus gives LIFE — not just eternal existence. He came into the world that we might have life and have it abundantly.

Eternal life is the gift of God: "For the wages of sin is death; **BUT THE GIFT OF GOD IS ETERNAL LIFE through Jesus Christ our Lord"** (Rom. 6:23). This is the verse used as a text the night God saved my poor, wretched, miserable soul. Through one hour of fervent, down-to-earth preaching the minister proved to me that I would

39

receive the wages of sin — **everlasting death.** He then held up to all unbelievers the gift of God — **eternal life** — and emphasized that eternal life is God's gift through the Lord Jesus Christ.

Just before Jesus bowed His thorn-crowned head and from the cross said, "Father, into thy hands I commend my Spirit," He cried out, "IT IS FINISHED!" (John 19: 30). The Lord Jesus Christ satisfied the heart of God, the righteousness of God, the holiness of God. Jesus took our place, He bore our sins in His own body on the cross (I Pet. 2:24).

A debt paid is no longer owed; it need not be paid but once. Jesus paid the sin-debt; therefore God gives to us eternal life when we receive the finished work of Jesus by faith. How wonderful is the gift God offers to all unbelievers — the gift of eternal life, the gift of Heaven! No one can buy the gift of God, and no one can earn it. Eternal life is a gift, and the only way to possess a gift is to receive it from the Giver. God **gave** Jesus, and when we **receive** Jesus, God gives us everlasting life.

Life eternal does not become ours through church membership or baptism, nor through good conduct or good living. God, and God alone, has made eternal life possible for all who will believe on the Lord Jesus Christ and receive Him by faith. Dear reader, are you saved? If you are not, will you accept Jesus now? Receive Him — **and thank God for life eternal!**

ONLY ONE WAY

John 3:16 is often referred to as "the Gospel in a nutshell." I suppose this verse has been memorized by more people than any other passage in all of the Word of God, except possibly the Twenty-Third Psalm.

To have eternal life we must be IN Christ: "There is therefore now no condemnation to them which are in Christ

Jesus" (Rom. 8:1a). "... Christ in you, the hope of glory." (Col. 1:27 b). "In Him was life; and the life was the light of men" (John 1:4).

To be IN CHRIST is to have life eternal; to be out of Christ is to be hopelessly lost. One cannot be saved by living a good life, nor is one lost because he lives a bad life. Mankind is saved or lost by receiving Christ or rejecting Him—there is no middle ground. We are either believers or unbelievers; we are either on the Lord's side, or else we are on the devil's side. Jesus said, "He that is not with me is against me" (Matt. 12:30).

"And this is the record, that God hath given to us eternal life, and this life is in His Son" (I John 5:11). Dear reader, can you see the truth of that verse from God's holy Word? "This IS the record." (That means it is finished, it is decided, and it has been recorded.) This is the divine fact that is recorded: "God hath GIVEN to us eternal life!"

Nothing could be clearer. This does not say that God has given us eternal life through baptism, through church membership, through good works, through moral living by doing the best we know how, or by living the best we can. It simply says that God HAS GIVEN to us eternal life. It is God's gift, not because of our merit or ability.

The last part of the verse clearly spells out what this life is, and where it is: "This life is IN HIS SON." The life God gives is not in the Church, it is not in the baptistry, it is not in good living, it is not in staying clean and pure. These are the results (or fruits) of salvation, but life eternal is in God's Son Jesus Christ. If you are in the Son, you are saved. If you are OUT of Christ, you are lost — even though you join every church on earth and be baptized in the river Jordan! You may live a clean, upright, holy life so far as these things are possible for man to perform; but unless you are in Christ, you are condemned and the

41

wrath of God hangs heavily over you this very moment. All a sinner need do — yea, all the sinner CAN do — to be saved is to believe on the Lord Jesus Christ and receive Him by faith.

ETERNAL LIFE A PRESENT POSSESSION

"He that believeth on the Son **HATH EVERLASTING LIFE**: and he that believeth not the Son shall not see life; but **THE WRATH OF GOD ABIDETH ON HIM**" (John 3:36).

"Verily, verily, I say unto you, He that believeth on me **HATH EVERLASTING LIFE**" (John 6:47).

These verses clearly state that those who have put their trust and faith in the finished work of the Lord Jesus Christ HAVE everlasting life — **present tense.** We who **believe** are saved NOW; we have eternal life NOW; we **ARE NOT** looking forward to a future date when we will **finally** possess eternal life. We have it now; we are sons of God NOW:

"Behold, what manner of love the Father hath bestowed upon us, that we should be called the sons of God: therefore the world knoweth us not, because it knew HIM not. Beloved, **NOW are we the sons of God,** and it doth not yet appear what we shall be: but we know that, when He shall appear, we shall be like Him; for we shall see Him as He is. And every man that hath this hope in him purifieth himself, even as He is pure" (I John 3:1-3). We have eternal life NOW. We are the sons of God NOW.

We possess divine nature NOW: "Whereby are given unto us exceeding great and precious promises: that by these ye might be partakers of the divine nature, having escaped the corruption that is in the world through lust" (II Pet. 1:4).

To believe on Christ is to **depend** upon Him — to save us, to make us sons of God, to give us life eternal. We do not believe on Christ and then **strive** to go to heaven; we believe on Him and **by faith** we go to heaven. Trusting in the finished work of Jesus, we have a sure passport to the Pearly White City.

To believe **ON Christ** is more than simply believing that there IS a Christ. We may drive our automobile up to a bridge, we may believe that it IS a bridge and that it was built in order that motorists might cross to the other side of the river; but we will never get across the stream as long as we sit in our car gazing at the bridge and believing that it IS a bridge which would support our automobile in crossing. We must believe ON the bridge — and when we believe on it, we drive our automobile onto the bridge and across the stream because we have faith that the bridge will hold us up out of the waters below which would destroy us. Believing on Jesus is to literally fling ourselves upon Him — soul, spirit, and body — depending upon Him for salvation, for eternal life — and **for victory in THIS life.**

Let me use another simple, down-to-earth illustration: No doubt many of you are presently sitting in a chair of one kind or another, and the reason you are sitting in that chair is because you believe ON it. You sat down upon it, you placed the weight of your body on the chair because you believe that it IS a chair and that it will support your body. Because of your faith in the chair you place your weight upon it. Sinner friend, if you will believe on Jesus in that very same way, He will save you this very moment!

THE PASSWORD TO HEAVEN

"Be it known unto you all, and to all the people of Israel, that by the name of Jesus Christ of Nazareth, whom ye crucified, whom God raised from the dead, even by Him doth this man stand here before you whole. This is the stone which was set at nought of you builders, which is become the head of the corner. Neither is there salvation in any other: **for there is none other name under heaven given among men, whereby we must be saved"** (Acts 4: 10-12).

Peter was preaching to the Sanhedrin when he gave this divine declaration. Israel had nailed Jesus of Nazareth to the cross — but God raised Him from the dead. Jesus is the stone which the builders set at nought; but God has made Him the head of the corner. "NEITHER IS THERE SALVATION IN ANY OTHER, for there is NONE OTHER NAME under heaven given among men, WHEREBY WE MUST BE SAVED!" There has never been but one name that would allow mankind to enter heaven, and that name is Jesus. He said, "I am the Door; by me if any man enter in, he shall be saved, and shall go in and out, and find pasture" (John 10:9).

Eternal life becomes ours through believing on the name of Jesus: "These things have I written unto you that believe on the name of the Son of God; that ye may know that ye have eternal life, and that ye may believe on the name of the Son of God" (I John 5:13).

The moment the unbeliever believes on Christ's name, eternal life becomes his:

"And she shall bring forth a Son, and thou shalt call His name JESUS: for He shall save His people from their sins" (Matt. 1:21).

"For whosoever shall call upon the name of the Lord shall be saved" (Rom. 10:13).

"He that beileveth on the Son hath everlasting life..." (John 3:36).

"He that hath the Son hath life..." (I John 5:12).

The same present possession is clearly set forth in John 3:16; 5-24; 6:47; and I John 5:11-13. Every person who from the heart believes on the name of the Lord Jesus

Christ has eternal life at this present moment. Eternal life is ours NOW.

WHAT IS ETERNAL LIFE?

I made the statement in the outset of this message that religion, denominations, and ministers have done a good job of confusing people, and I will stand by that statement. Denominational terms are confusing; **Bible** terms are **never** confusing. The Word of God is written in simple, understandable language.

The sermons Jesus preached were "down-to-earth" — so much so that He talked about the seed, the sower, the good ground, the thorny ground. He talked about sparrows, lilies of the field, the hen and her chicks. He talked of light, water, salt, and bread. Who could not understand these simple words? And yet today, for some reason which I have never been able to understand, ministers of the Gospel seem to find great joy and a "pulpit thrill" in using great, swelling words to advertise their seminary training!

I am not against education — a young man who is too lazy to go to school is not fit to preach, and by like token, a **young lady** who is too lazy to go to school is not fit to serve on the mission field. But education that removes the simplicity of the Gospel is not **Christian education.**

What is eternal life? Let Jesus answer: **"And I give unto them eternal life; and they shall never perish, neither shall any man pluck them out of my hand"** (John 10:28). According to these words, Jesus not only GIVES us eternal life, but He gives us life that will never perish. Christ IS our life, He is our hope. Christ is our assurance, He is our security. I have Christ and I have His Word — what more do I need? I believe the Word of God simply **because it IS the Word of God.**

Hear these tremendous truths clearly set forth:

"There is therefore now no condemnation to them which

are in Christ Jesus, who walk not after the flesh, but after the Spirit. For the law of the Spirit of life in Christ Jesus hath made me free from the law of sin and death. For what the law could not do, in that it was weak through the flesh, God sending His own Son **in the likeness** of sinful flesh, and for sin, condemned sin in the flesh... But ye are not in the flesh, but in the Spirit, if so be that the Spirit of God dwell in you. Now if any man have not the Spirit of Christ, he is none of His. And if Christ be in you, the body is dead because of sin but the Spirit is life because of righteousness... For as many as are led by the Spirit of God, they are the sons of God... The Spirit itself beareth witness with our spirit, that we are the children of God... What shall we then say to these things? If God be for us, who can be against us? He that spared not His own Son, but delivered Him up for us all, how shall He not with Him also freely give us all things? Who shall lay anything to the charge of God's elect? It is God that justifieth. Who is he that condemneth? It is Christ that died, yea rather, that is risen again, who is even at the right hand of God, who also maketh intercession for us. Who shall separate us from the love of Christ? shall tribulation, or distress, or persecution, or famine, or nakedness, or peril, or sword? As it is written, For thy sake we are killed all the day long; we are accounted as sheep for the slaughter. Nay, in all these things we are more than conquerors through Him that loved us. For I am persuaded, that neither death, nor life, nor angels, nor principalities, nor powers, nor things present, nor things to come, nor height, nor depth, **nor any other creature, shall be able to separate us from the love of God which is in Christ Jesus our Lord"** (Rom. 8:1-39 in part).

The eighth chapter of Romans is one of my favorite passages in all of the Bible because it BEGINS in Jesus and CLOSES in Jesus. Here is what I mean:

Verse 1: "There is therefore now no condemnation to them which are **IN CHRIST JESUS...**"

Verse 39: "Nor height, nor depth, nor any other creature, shall be able to separate us from the love of God, which is **IN CHRIST JESUS** our Lord!"

So you see, beloved, MAN is out of it. Salvation **begins** in Jesus, **continues** in Jesus, and **climaxes** in Jesus. We look unto Him, the author and finisher of our faith (Heb. 12:2).

Eternal life is in Christ. Not only is eternal life IN Christ, but eternal life IS Christ! Many dear people think of eternal life in terms of length of years, but this is only one small phase of it. All unbelievers who die in sin will live eternally, but they will not have life; they will have death — **ETERNAL death in the lake of fire.** There will be no end to the punishment of the unbeliever, he will live on and on — and everlastingly he will be tormented! The hottest, most scorching sermon ever preached on hell was preached by none other than the gentle, compassionate, loving Son of God. You can almost smell the sulphur as you read it! (Mark 9:42 ff). Sinner friend, **read that sermon:** then re-read it — and **read it again!!!**

Now — if eternal life is merely a matter of duration of years, ungodly sinners would also have eternal life; but such is not the case according to the Word of God. Eternal life is much, much more than duration of years: **eternal life is the very life of Christ** — in the believer NOW and continuing in the believer until he goes to be with Christ or until Christ comes in the Rapture. HE is eternal life, He IS our life, and to have HIM is to **have** eternal life.

Have you ever heard it said of one who suffered severely and for a long period of time before departing this life, "He died a dozen deaths"? That statement is often used in reference to a person who dies slowly, painfully, day by day and hour by hour while the heart continues to beat. Such an individual often begs — yea, **prays** — for death, and would welcome it.

Eternal life is more than everlasting existence: **It is the life of God in YOU NOW,** and continuing in you throughout eternity. After the Rapture we will live in a body just like the resurrection body of Jesus. Those who have died in the Lord are resting (Rev. 14:13); but they do not yet have their glorified bodies. We will be like Jesus when we see Him as He is, when this mortal puts on immortality. When the dead in Christ are raised incorruptible they will have glorified bodies that will never be sick, but the life of Christ will continue to live in that glorified body — yes, in our own personality-but life eternal is Christ, and Christ alone.

THE WAY — THE TRUTH — THE LIFE

In John 13 Jesus told His disciples that He would journey to Jerusalem, and there He would be arrested, tried, condemned — and put to death. That broke their hearts and left them sad and troubled. Jesus knew this, and He said to the troubled disciples, "Let not your heart be troubled: ye believe in God, believe also in me. In my Father's house are many mansions: If it were not so, I would have told you. I go to prepare a place for you. And if I go and prepare a place for you, I will come again, and receive you unto myself that where I am, there ye may be also. And whither I go ye know, and the way ye know. Thomas saith unto Him, Lord, we know not whither thou goest; and how can we know the way? Jesus saith unto him, I am the way, the truth, and the life: NO MAN COMETH UNTO THE FATHER, BUT BY ME" (John 14:1-6).

Thomas is known as "doubting Thomas," but I thank God for the question he asked here and which Jesus answered, because without the Way, there is no going; without the Truth, there is no knowing; without the life, there is no living. Jesus is the Way, Jesus is the Truth that sets men free, and Jesus is the Life:

"And this is life eternal, that they might know thee the only true God, and Jesus Christ, whom thou hast sent" (John 17:3). What is eternal life? Is it joining the church? Is it being baptized? Is it living the best we know how? NO! THIS is life eternal: **"That they might know thee, the only true God, and Jesus Christ."** Jesus Christ is eternal life.

There was a humble little home in Bethany. Mary, Martha, and Lazarus lived there, and Jesus loved to visit in that home. Those dear people had warm hearts and they made Him welcome. It is true that He was God Almighty in flesh — but He was also man. He had a heart that felt how people felt toward Him when He was in their presence. Mary, Martha, and Lazarus loved Him — and He knew it.

Jesus was away on a preaching mission, Lazarus was sick, and his sisters sent word to Jesus saying, "Lord, he whom thou lovest is sick." But Jesus did not return to Bethany immediately. Four days later he returned — but Lazarus was dead and in the tomb. Martha went out to meet the Lord, "but Mary sat still in the house, Then said Martha unto Jesus, Lord, if thou hadst been here, my brother had not died." But Jesus replied, **"I am the resurrection, and the life:** he that believeth in me, though he were dead, yet shall he live: And whosoever liveth and believeth in me shall never die" (John 11:25, 26).

These words are easily understood by those who are not married to some religion or cult. Lazarus was dead, four days in the grave — his body had begun to decay; but Jesus said, "I am the resurrection ... I am the life ... He that believeth in me..." Simple, is it not? He said, "I

AM..." Jesus is all that God requires: He is all that we need. He is the way, He is the truth, He is the life, He is the resurrection.

In Colossians 3:4 we read, "When Christ, who is our life, shall appear, then shall ye also appear with Him in glory." So simple; so clear and understandable. How can anyone miss it? "When Christ WHO IS OUR LIFE..." Christ is our life — not church membership, not baptism, not good works, not giving our money. Christ is our life, and "WHEN HE SHALL APPEAR....." He is coming. He said, "I go away, I will come again." And when He comes, **we will appear with Him in glory.**

"And this is the record, that God hath given to us eternal life, and this life is in His Son" (I John 5:11).

"This then is the message which we have heard of Him, and declare unto you, that God is life, and in Him is no darkness at all. If we say that we have fellowship with Him, and walk in darkness, we lie, and do not the truth: But if we walk in the light, as He is in the light, we have fellowship one with another, and the blood of Jesus Christ His Son cleanseth us from all sin" (I John 1:5-7).

"And this is the confidence that we have in Him, that, if we ask any thing according to His will, He heareth us: And if we know that He hear us, whatsoever we ask, we know that we have the petitions that we desired of Him" (I John 5:14, 15).

ENTICING WORDS ARE DANGEROUS

"And this I say, lest any man should beguile you with enticing words. For though I be absent in the flesh, yet am I with you in the spirit, joying and beholding your order, and the stedfastness of your faith in Christ. As ye have therefore received Christ Jesus the Lord, so walk ye in Him: Rooted and built up in Him, and stablished in the faith, as ye have been taught, abounding therein with thanksgiving. Beware lest any man spoil you through philosophy and vain deceit, after the tradition of men, after the rudiments of the world, and not after Christ. For in Him dwelleth all the fulness of the Godhead bodily. And ye are complete in Him, which is the head of all principality and power:" (What can be added to **fulness**? What can be added to **completeness**?) "In whom also ye are circumcised with the circumcison made without hands, in putting off the body of the sins of the flesh by the circumcision of Christ: Buried with Him in baptism, wherein also ye are risen with Him through the faith of the operation of God, who hath raised Him from the dead. And you, being dead in your sins and the uncircumcision of your flesh, hath He quickened together with Him, having forgiven you all trespasses; blotting out the handwriting of ordinances that was against us, and took it out of the way, nailing it to His cross; and having spoiled principalities and powers, He made a shew of them openly, triumphing over them in it" (Col. 2:4-15).

Paul was jealous for Jesus. His determination was to know nothing save Jesus Christ, crucified, risen, and coming again ("according to the Scriptures") all-sufficient ("according to the Scriptures"). And He declared, "But though we, or an angel from heaven, preach any other gospel unto you than that which we have preached unto you, let him be accursed" (Gal. 1:8).

Do you, dear reader, have eternal life? Or do you just have "religion" or church membership? Are you one of those who say, "I am living the very best I know how?" If you do not know beyond the shadow of a doubt that you are saved now, then according to the Scripture **you are lost now**! If you are truly born again, you KNOW it; and if you do NOT know you are saved, I plead with you to receive Jesus by faith this very moment, **and He will save you NOW.**

"That if thou shalt confess with thy mouth the Lord Jesus, and shalt believe in thine heart that God hath raised Him from the dead, thou shalt be saved. For with the heart man believeth unto righteousness; and with the mouth confession is made unto salvation" (Rom. 10:9, 10).

The Bible Assurance of What Believers Are

THE BIBLE ASSURANCE
OF WHAT BELIEVERS ARE

The subject of the assurance of salvation is a vital and most important one. It has much to do with the peace and joy of the Christian, because no person can enjoy his spiritual birthright apart from the assurance of salvation. There are many professing Christians who do not know definitely and assuredly that they are saved. Ministers have sadly neglected this important subject which so vitally concerns the souls of men; and I believe there are rare cases where people are truly saved, yet for lack of instruction in the Word, there are times of physical weakness or mental strain when they may momentarily doubt their salvation.

For many years I have been asking people, "Are you saved?" and often the answer is, "I think so . . . I hope so . . . I am doing the very best I know how." Or perhaps they reply, "I am living the very best I can." Some will say, "I do not know," while still others will say, "I do not believe we can know the answer to that question until we die."

These vague answers reveal the distressing, heart-sickening truth that there are thousands of church members who know nothing of the assurance of salvation. But there are a few who grip my hand firmly and with clear, honest gaze answer, "YES, I AM SAVED!"

It is the spiritual birthright of every child of God to know beyond a shadow of doubt that he or she is saved. *Doubt* is the work of the Christian's adversary, the devil. Satan is a powerful creature and seems to influence many church people to the extent that they believe him when he tells them they are lost, or that they have never really been saved. This is the language he uses when attempting to cause a truly born again Christian to doubt his salvation—and sometimes in moments of weakness he wins a momentary victory! On the other hand, he tells many church people who are NOT born again that there is really nothing to worry about.

Satan is a liar. He is the father of lies; in him the lie was born. He is a thief, a murderer the archenemy of every person alive—saint or sinner. If he cannot damn a soul, then his one desire is to rob that soul of its spiritual birthright—which is the positive assurance of salvation, (with joy unspeakable and full of glory), and peace that passes all understanding. Certainly if the devil can cause a true Christian to doubt his salvation, he has won a tremendous victory over that Christian, because a believer is of no earthly good to the cause of Christ if within his own heart there is misery instead of peace.

In my revival meetings in the past few years I have observed that it is usually the same group who come forward from time to time for prayer. There are new ones occasionally, but the majority of those who come forward for prayer are already members of the church. I personally believe that this is evidence that Satan is working overtime today to cause believers to doubt their salvation, and by so doing he causes them to be fruitless in winning others to Jesus.

So often we hear someone pray a flowery, beautiful prayer—and then close with these words: *"At last save us all in heaven. Amen."* Such a statement is due to Bible ignorance, and instead of helping, it *hurts* the cause of Christ. If the person praying that prayer is really born again, he does not have the assurance of salvation, and such a prayer will not help others to be assured of their salvation. The Bible does not teach that we must wait

56

until we die to know whether or not we are saved. The Bible does not teach us to pray "Lord, at last save us in heaven." The Bible teaches us, "Today is the day of salvation. NOW is the accepted time." And if we are saved NOW we do not need to pray "Lord save us at last when we reach heaven." Thank God, we can know NOW —yea, this very second we can know that we are genuinely born again.

Many church people do not have Bible assurance of salvation because they trust in *"feelings."* It is a sad, heartbreaking fact that many church people put their trust in feelings rather than in the Word of God. *Feeling* is more real and means more to them than *"Thus saith the Lord!"* It is not *feeling* that saves us; it is the blood of Jesus Christ that washes away our sins. Feelings vary from day to day, or even hour by hour. Feelings come from emotions; but *faith dwells in the heart.*

". . . With the heart man believeth unto righteousness; and with the mouth confession is made unto salvation" (Rom. 10:10). There is no verse—nor part of a verse— in God's holy Word that so much as indicates, "By *feelings* you are saved, through emotion." Feelings have nothing to do with salvation. It is true that peace comes into our heart when we are born again, but peace is not necessarily emotion. There are dear Christians who suffer severely in body and in mind, yet have unshakeable confidence in the heart. *They know whom they have believed,* and are persuaded that He is able to keep that which they have committed unto Him against that day.

God pity the poor church member who trusts in feelings. I do not discount the fact that some church people appear to be very happy. They appear to feel beyond the average believer's understanding. Many clap their hands, wave their arms, and shout; but this does not necessarily mean that they are saved. Outward demonstration of emotion does not prove inward possession of the grace of God.

However, salvation is not *totally apart* from emotion. When God saves us, we receive the Holy Spirit, we have the peace of God, we receive a new heart and *we become a new creation in Christ*. There is a definite change in the inner man, but this change does not always produce the same outward effect in all converts. It does not always produce either tears, smiles, excitement or shouts of joy. It DOES bring peace, gladness, and assurance to the heart. There is no Scripture in all the Bible that will tell you that you are saved because you FEEL saved. On the the contrary, there are many Scriptures which clearly teach that we are saved because we believe in the finished work of Jesus and trust in His blood.

Jesus said, "Verily, verily, I say unto you, He that heareth my word, and believeth on Him that sent me, hath everlasting life, and shall not come into condemnation, but is passed from death unto life" (John 5:24). Dear reader, if you are a doubter, may God help you never to doubt His Word again. Believe God—for "he that doubteth is damned," and *"whatsoever is not of faith is sin"* (Rom. 14:23).

To doubt God's Word is to make God a liar. Divorce yourself from your doubt, from "feeling," and put complete confidence in the finished work of Jesus, the shed blood of His cross and the testimony of God's Word.

There are many things in the Bible that I do not fully understand, but *I do know for sure that I am a child of God!* Assurance is mine because of three things:

1. I know I am saved through *the testimony of the Word of God.* The Word clearly tells me what I must do to be

saved. I have done that, and I am standing on God's Word. (I had a million times rather stand on the Word than to stand on my feelings.)

2. I know I am saved because *of the testimony of the Spirit*. The Bible tells me, "The Spirit itself beareth witness with our spirit, that we are the children of God" (Rom. 8:16). I know I am a child of God because I have the witness of the Spirit in my heart to lead, guide, and assure me.

3. I know I am saved because *my heart condemns me not*. John tells us, "Hereby we know that we are of the truth, and shall assure our hearts before Him. For if our heart condemn us, God is greater than our heart, and knoweth all things. Beloved if our heart condemn us not, then have we confidence toward God" (I John 3:19-21). In the early hours of morning, in the dark hours of the night, or in the brightness of noonday, I can ask my heart, "Am I really a child of God?" And my heart replies "Yes!" in a voice not heard by mortal ear but recognized by the regenerated heart. I know I am saved because my heart leads me to "do those things that are pleasing in His sight." I love to work for Jesus, whereas when I was an unbeliever I took great joy in serving Satan.

We can know we are children of God through *the Word of God,* through the *witness of the Spirit of God,* and through *the work of God in our hearts and lives.*

WHAT WE ARE NOW

I want us to have the assurance of what we are *right now*—not what we *will be* at the end of life's journey or on the great judgment morning.

1. *We are SAVED now*:

"For the preaching of the cross is to them that perish foolishness; but unto us which *are saved* it is the power of God" (I Cor: 1:18). Please note the language used here. Paul did not say, ". . . Unto us which *will be* saved in the end . . . Unto us who *hope* we are saved . . . Unto us who *think* we are saved." He makes a positive, clear-cut statement: *"Unto us which ARE Saved."* We are not BEING saved, *we are saved NOW*.

In II Timothy 1: 9 and 10 Paul said, "Who HATH saved us, and called us with an holy calling, not according to our works, but according to His own purpose and grace, which was given us in Christ Jesus before the world began but is NOW made manifest by the appearing of our Saviour Jesus Christ, who HATH abolished death, and HATH brought life and immortality to light through the Gospel."

Again the statement is plain: *"Who HATH saved us."* This is past tense—God saved us when we believed on Jesus Christ, and called us with an holy calling. It was Jesus who, through the blood of His cross, has saved us and called us—not by works of righteousness which we have done, nor by works which we can or *will do*. We are saved the second we embrace the finished work of Jesus by faith. We are saved NOW—and we will be saved in His presence when He comes for His Church.

"Not by works of righteousness which we have done, but according to His mercy He saved us, by the washing of regeneration, and renewing of the Holy Ghost" (Tit. 3:5). So clear, so plain, so understandable! how could anyone miss it? We are saved—not by the washing of the baptistry, not by good works, but by the washing of regeneration and the renewing of the Holy Ghost.

These precious Scriptures are very clear on the assurance of salvation. We who are saved are not children of God because we FEEL saved, but because we have received the

Lord Jesus Christ and trusted in His Word. "The entrance of thy words giveth light" (Psalm 119:130). "Thy Word is a lamp unto my feet, and a light unto my path" (Psalm 119:105). Light illumines. Light gives us a sure footing. Truly born again believers have the Light burning in their soul. What more could God say, what more could He do, to give us assurance? If we refuse to believe His Word and stand on "Thus saith the Lord" how could we hope to have assurance through any feeling or emotion that we might experience through the energy of the flesh?

2. *We have the assurance that SIN IS FORGIVEN*:

It is sin (singular) that damns the soul—not sins (plural). In John 3:18 we read, "He that believeth on Him is not condemned: but he that believeth not is *condemned already*, because he *hath not believed* in the name of the only begotten Son of God." In this tremendous verse, three things are clearly set forth:

Believers are *not* condemned.

Unbelievers ARE condemned —

Because they believe not on the name of the Son of God.

The sin of unbelief has damned every soul that is tormented in the flames of hell today, and unbelief will damn every soul that drops into the pit from this moment until the consummation of all things.

John the Baptist said, "Behold the Lamb of God, which taketh away the *sin* of the world" (John 1:29). Please note that the word used here is S-I-N, singular; not S-I-N-S, plural. Jesus enlarges upon this truth in John 16:7-11:

"Nevertheless I tell you the truth: It is expedient for you that I go away: for if I go not away, the Comforter will not come unto you; but if I depart, I will send Him unto you. And when He is come, He will reprove the world *of SIN,* and of righteousness, and of judgment: *OF SIN, because they believe not on me;* Of righteousness, because I go to my Father, and ye see me no more; Of judgment, because the prince of this world is judged."

Please notice again—it is S-I-N (singular) because they believe not on Jesus. Drinking, gambling, lying, stealing, murder, adultery and all other sins catalogued are simply *fruits* of the damning *SIN of unbelief.* The sinner need only pray, "God, be merciful to me, a sinner." SIN is *forgiven* when we believe on the Lord Jesus Christ. SINS should be *confessed:* ". . . . And if any man sin, we have an Advocate with the Father, Jesus Christ the righteous" (I John 2:1-b). "If we confess our sins, He is faithful and just to forgive us our sins, and to cleanse us from all unrighteousness (I John 1:9).

S-I-N (singular) damns the sinner; S-I-N-S (plural) rob the Christian. Believers have been forgiven SIN, SIN is covered by the blood; and when we are covered by the blood of Jesus, then in the sight of God Almighty we are just as pure as the blood that covers us.

3. *Believers are JUSTIFIED now:*

"Therefore being justified by faith, we have peace with God through our Lord Jesus Christ" (Rom. 5-1).

We are justified by faith in the finished work of Jesus Christ; and since we ARE justified, we are assured that by and through the Lord Jesus we have access into the grace of God—and God's grace is sufficient for any and all needs, here and hereafter. Being justified, we "rejoice in hope of the glory of God . . . we glory in tribulation also, knowing that tribulation worketh patience; and patience, experience; and experience, hope; and hope maketh not ashamed; because the love of God is shed abroad in our hearts by the Holy Ghost which is given unto us."

"Much more then, *being NOW justified by His blood,* we shall be saved from wrath through him!" Paul climaxed this glorious truth with these glorious words: "And not only so, but we also joy in God through our Lord Jesus Christ, by whom *we have NOW received the atonement*" (Rom. 5:2-11 in part).

Please notice: Justification is ours NOW. We are NOW justified by His blood. We have the atonement NOW: ". . . By whom we have NOW received the atonement." Thank God for the unshakeable assurance that we are saved, our sin is forgiven and covered by the blood, we are justified by faith through the blood of Jesus, and at this very moment we have the atonement.

4. *Believers are SANCTIFIED now:*

The very instant an unbeliever is converted, he is sanctified *positionally*. He is translated from the kingdom of darkness into the kingdom of light:

"Giving thanks unto the Father, which hath made us meet to be partakers of the inheritance of the saints in light: who hath delivered us from the power of darkness, and hath translated us into the kingdom of His dear Son" (Col. 1:12, 13).

When we believe on the Lord Jesus Christ, we are translated from the kingdom of Satan (darkness) into the kingdom of God's dear son (the kingdom of light). Positionally we are sanctified, set apart, from the kingdom of darkness.

HOW are we sanctified? I Corinthians 1:29-31 answers: *"That no flesh should glory in His presence.* But of Him are ye in Christ Jesus, who of God is made unto us wisdom, and righteousness, and SANCTIFICATION, and redemption: That, according as it is written, He that glorieth, let him glory in the Lord!"

Christ is our sanctification. In the Lord's prayer of intercession, just before He went to the cross, He prayed, "Father . . . *SANCTIFY them through thy truth: thy Word is truth.* As thou hast sent me into the world, even so have I also sent them into the world. And for their sakes I SANCTIFY myself, that they also might be *SANCTIFIED through the truth.* Neither pray I for these alone, but for them also which shall believe on me through their word; that they all may be one; as thou, Father, art in me, and I in thee, that they also may be one in us: that the world may believe that thou hast sent me" (John 17:17-21).

All believers are sanctified: "Wherefore when He cometh into the world, He saith, Sacrifice and offering thou wouldest not, but a body hast thou prepared me: In burnt-offerings and sacrifices for sin thou hast had no pleasure. Then said I, Lo, I come (in the volume of the book it is written of me,) to do thy will, O God. Above when He said, Sacrifice and offering and burnt-offerings and offering for sin thou wouldest not, neither hadst pleasure therein; which are offered by the law; Then said He, Lo, I come to do thy will, O God. He taketh away the first, that He may establish the second. By the which will *we are SANCTIFIED through the offering of the body of Jesus Christ once for all.* And every priest standeth daily ministering and offering oftentimes the same sacrifices, which can never take away sins: But this man (Jesus), after He had offered one sacrifice for sins for ever, sat down on the right hand of God; From henceforth expecting till His enemies be made His footstool. *For by one*

offering He hath perfected for ever them that are SANC-
TIFIED" (Heb. 10:5-14).

These verses speak for themselves, but I would emphasize the glorious truth that all who believe on the Lord
Jesus are sanctified because we are in Him (Col. 3:3) and
He is in us (Col. 1:27). The salvation that is ours through
faith in the shed blood of Jesus Christ provides sanctification through the one offering of Jesus—His blood, shed
on the cross; and by this one offering *He has perfected*
FOREVER them that are SANCTIFIED. That's good
enough for me! Hallelujah!

5. *Believers are PRESERVED now:*

"And the very God of peace sanctify you wholly; and
I pray God your whole spirit and soul and body be
PRESERVED blameless unto the coming of our Lord
Jesus Christ" (I Thess. 5:23).

These are tremendous words — note them carefully:
Paul prayed that God would sanctify the Thessalonian
believers *wholly*—meaning *"entirely."* He did not suggest
that they sanctify *themselves,* but that GOD sanctify them;
and that they be *PRESERVED—soul, spirit, and body,*
blameless, UNTIL JESUS COMES!

God *saves the soul* the split second we are born again.
He *sanctifies* us the split second we are born again. But
Paul wanted the believers PRESERVED until Jesus comes.

I love words. I *study* words. The Bible is THE WORD
of God—a book composed of sixty-six books, many chapters, thousands of verses, and tens of thousands of words.
Yet every word has a meaning. No words were put in
the Bible just to fill up space. The word "preserved" has
tremendous meaning. Paul said, "preserved *blameless,"*
not "sinless perfect." (The soul and spirit are sinless perfect, but the *body* will be weak and faulty until we are
changed and made like unto Jesus' glorious resurrection

body.) But we can live a *blameless* life, we *should* live a blameless life, PRESERVED in the grace of God!

I am afraid the reason so many church members spoil so easily and so often is that they are *"canned* in religion" instead of being *"preserved* in the grace of God." In Jude, verses 1 and 2, we read, "Jude, the servant of Jesus Christ, and brother of James, to them that are sanctified by God the Father, and PRESERVED in Jesus Christ, and called: Mercy unto you, and peace, and love, be multiplied."

6. *Believers are KEPT now*:

Many weary sinners want to be saved, they shudder at the thought of burning in hell. They say, "I would become a Christian if I only knew that I could live a Christian life and not slip back into the world." Such a statement is due to Bible ignorance—and Bible ignorance is many times due to neglect of ministers to teach the Word. God's Word clearly teaches us that *"He which hath begun a good work in you will perform it until the day of Jesus Christ!"* (Phil. 1:6).

The only possible way for any person to live a victorious Christian life is by faith: "Whosoever believeth that Jesus is the Christ is born of God: and every one that loveth Him that begat loveth Him also that is begotten of Him . . . For whatsoever is born of God overcometh the world: and this is the victory that overcometh the world, even our faith. Who is he that overcometh the world, but he that believeth that Jesus is the Son of God?" (I John 5:1-5 in part). FAITH is the victory that overcomes the world!

"What shall we then say to these things? If God be for us, who can be against us? . . . Who shall separate us from the love of Christ? Shall tribulation, or distress, or persecution, or famine, or nakedness, or peril, or sword? As it is written, For thy sake we are killed all the day long; we are accounted as sheep for the slaughter. Nay, IN

ALL THESE THINGS WE ARE MORE THAN CON-
QUERORS THROUGH HIM THAT LOVED US. For I
am persuaded, that neither death, nor life, nor angels, nor
principalities, nor powers, nor things present, nor things to
come, nor height, nor depth, NOR ANY OTHER CREA-
TURE, shall be able to separate us from the love of God,
which is in Christ Jesus our Lord" (Rom. 8:31, 35-39).

We are MORE than conquerors—but only in the Lord
Jesus Christ. He conquered the world, the flesh, the devil,
death, hell, and the grave; and the only way *we* can conquer
is in Him.

"Blessed be the God and Father of our Lord Jesus Christ,
which according to His abundant mercy hath begotten us
again unto a lively (living) hope by the resurrection of
Jesus Christ from the dead, *to an inheritance incorruptible,
undefiled, and that fadeth not away, reserved in heaven
for you, who are KEPT BY THE POWER OF GOD
THROUGH FAITH unto salvation ready to be revealed
in the last time"* (I Pet. 1:3-5).

We are *saved* by God's grace through faith. Salvation
is the gift of God—we cannot save ourselves. By like
token, we are KEPT by the power of God. We can no
more *keep ourselves* than we can *save* ourselves. But thank
God, through His keeping power we have victory NOW—
we are not just looking forward to victory at some time
in the future. He who has begun a good work in us will
perform it. He has promised never to leave us nor forsake
us, " . . . so that we may boldly say, The Lord is my
helper, and I will not fear what man shall do unto me"
(Heb. 13.6). He will go with us all the way, even unto
the end.

7. *Believers are COMPLETE now:*

"Beware lest any man spoil you through philosophy
and vain deceit, after the tradition of men, after the rudi-

ments of the world, and not after Christ. For in Him dwelleth all the fulness of the Godhead bodily. *And ye are COMPLETE IN HIM, which is the head of all principality and power"* (Col. 2:8-10).

What can be added to completeness? In Jesus we live and move and have our being. He is our salvation, our righteousness, our hope. He is our all in all. We are in Him, He is in us. We sit together in heavenly places in Christ Jesus, and *we are complete in Him.*

When God saves the sinner the transaction is perfect *because God is perfect.* The salvation we enjoy was provided by Him and He does not leave any untied ends, any broken threads, any pieces that do not fit together in perfect harmony. Whatsoever God does He does perfectly, because God could do nothing *less* than perfect.

God so loved the world that He gave Jesus. Jesus was heaven's best given for earth's worst. Just before He went to the cross He prayed to the heavenly Father, "If it be POSSIBLE, let this cup pass." But it was not possible —*it had to be Jesus.* What God demands, God provides. Only God could provide righteousness, holiness, and purity. These He provided in Jesus, and in HIM we are complete.

8. *Believers are IN CHRIST now:*

"For as the body is one, and hath many members, and all the members of that one body, being many, are one body: so also is Christ. For by one Spirit are we all baptized into one body, whether we be Jews or Gentiles, whether we be bond or free; and have been all made to drink into one Spirit. For the body is not one member, but many" (I Cor. 12:12-14).

The same truth is set forth in Ephesians 5:22-27: "Wives, submit yourselves unto your own husbands, as unto the Lord. For the husband is the head of the wife, *even as Christ is the head of the Church: and He is the*

Saviour of the body. Therefore as the Church is subject unto Christ, so let the wives be to their own husbands in every thing. Husbands, love your wives, *even as Christ also loved the Church, and gave Himself for it;* that He might sanctify and cleanse it with the washing of water by the Word, that He might present it to Himself a glorious Church not having spot, or wrinkle, or any such thing; but that it should be holy and without blemish."

Paul illustrates the relationship of Christ and the Church by using husband and wife. Every born again, blood-washed child of God *is now* baptized into the body of Christ: *"For we are members of His body, of His flesh, and of His bones"* (Eph. 5:30).

What a glorious revelation! What a comforting fact! We are now bone of HIS bone, flesh of HIS flesh. We are IN JESUS, in the body, the New Testament Church—through the baptism of the Holy Spirit which occurs the moment we believe. We are born of the Spirit, united to the body of Christ by the Spirit, indwelt by the Spirit, led by the Spirit, assured by the Spirit, and SEALED by the Spirit. We are NOW in His body—literally a part of His flesh and of His bones!

THE ONENESS OF CHRIST AND THE BELIEVER

I would emphasize this tremendous truth: The Word of God declares that Christ and His people are ONE: "For both He that sanctifieth and they who are sanctified ARE ALL OF ONE" (Heb. 2:11). Again, "He that is joined unto the Lord is ONE SPIRIT" (I Cor. 6:17). "God is faithful, by whom ye were called unto the fellowship (partnership) of His Son Jesus Christ our Lord" (I Cor. 1:9) ". . . As He is, so are we in this world" (I John 4:17). And finally, ". . . And we are IN HIM" (I John 5:20). Praise God for the oneness of the believer and the Christ in whom we believe!

I believe in Bible election and Bible predestination. I believe in the sovereignty of God and the foreknowledge of God. I confess I do not understand these tremendous truths, but I believe them because they are the Word of God. I know that God knows the end in the begining, and He knows all that lies *between* the beginning and the end. The Scriptures teach, ". . . He hath chosen us in Him before the foundation of the world . . ." (Eph. 1:4) ; therefore, *the oneness of Christ and the Christian has existed (and will continue to exist) eternally.*

". . . He hath chosen US . . ." referring to all saints—the New Testament Church. It is true that the CHURCH was chosen, foreordained, and elected—but *individuals* become members of that body through their own desire, of their own free will. Jesus said to His own people, "And *ye will not* come to me, that ye might have life" (John 5:40). On another occasion, as He wept over the Holy City, He said "O Jerusalem, Jerusalem, which killest the prophets, and stonest them that are sent unto thee; how often would I have gathered thy children, together, as a hen doth gather her brood under her wings, and *YE WOULD NOT!*" (Luke 13:34).

I believe in Bible election—but I also believe in John 3:16: "For God so loved the world, that He gave His only begotten Son, that *WHOSOEVER believeth in Him* should not perish, but have everlasting life!"

Paul speaks of "the mystery, which from the beginning of the world hath been hid in God" (Eph. 3.9). This is the mystery of Jew and Gentile, slave and master, (*"whosoever"*) in ONE BODY by grace through faith in the shed blood of Jesus. God gave Paul the revelation of this mystery that he might make known the grace of God—and he did just that, preaching salvation for "whosoever will"—but only by grace through faith.

God the Father has given God the Son, that we might be ONE with Him. The only begotten Son of God left the Father's bosom and came to earth. God gave Him a body of flesh in order that He might be as we are, except for His sinlessness.

"Forasmuch then as the children are partakers of flesh and blood, He also Himself likewise took part of the same; that through death He might destroy Him that had the power of death, that is, the devil; and deliver them who through fear of death were all their lifetime subject to bondage" (Heb. 2:14, 15).

Earthly children are partakers of the flesh and blood of their parents. Jesus took the flesh part of man, but His blood was given to Him by God the Father: Acts 20: 28 mentions "the Church of God, *which He hath purchased with His own blood.*" The blood that flowed in the veins of Jesus was divine.

Not only did Jesus become one with us in that He became the Son of man, having received His flesh from the virgin Mary, but He also became *one with us in our sins*—that is, He took our sins and confessed them to the heavenly Father as His very own:

"For innumerable evils have compassed me about: *mine iniquities* have taken hold upon me, so that I am not able to look up; they are more than the hairs of mine head: therefore my heart faileth me!" (Psalm 40:12).

Isaiah tells us, "Surely He hath borne our griefs, and carried our sorrows: yet we did esteem Him stricken, smitten of God, and afflicted. But He was wounded for *our* transgressions, He was bruised for *our iniquities,* the chastisement of *our* peace was upon Him! and with HIS stripes WE are healed" (Isa. 53:4, 5).

"When the even was come, they brought unto Him many that were possessed with devils: and He cast out the spirits with His word, and healed all that were sick: That it might be fulfilled which was spoken by Esaias the prophet, saying, *Himself took our infirmities, and bare our sickness*" (Matt. 8:16, 17).

"Who *His own self* bare OUR sins in His own body on the tree, that we, being dead to sins, should live unto righteousness: by whose stripes ye were healed" (I Pet. 2:24).

On the cross, Jesus manifested this divine oneness which we now possess with Him: "Knowing this, that our old man is crucified with Him, that the body of sin might be destroyed, that henceforth, we should not serve sin" (Rom. 6:6).

Paul said, "I am crucified with Christ: nevertheless I live; yet not I, but Christ liveth in me: and the life which I now live in the flesh I live by the faith of the Son of God, who loved me, and gave Himself for me" (Gal. 2:20). Paul was alive—yet he was dead to the "old man," dead to the world, dead to sin—but alive unto God. So is every born again believer. We are *one with Jesus in death and burial*:

"Therefore we are buried with Him by baptism into death: that like as Christ was raised up from the dead by the glory of the Father, even so we also should walk in newness of life. For if we have been planted together in the likeness of His death, we shall be also in the likeness of His resurrection: Knowing this, that our old man is crucified with Him, that the body of sin might be destroyed, that henceforth we should not serve sin" (Rom.6:4-6).Believers are made ONE with Jesus *in life.*We are made alive together with Jesus in God: "But God, who is rich in mercy, for His great love wherewith He loved us, even when we were dead in sins, hath quickened us together with Christ . . ." (Eph. 2:4, 5). All unbelievers are dead in trespasses and sins (Eph. 2:1); and the wages of sin is death (Rom. 6:23) ; but when we believe on the Lord Jesus Christ, we are quickened and made alive—made ONE with Him.

Believers are one with Jesus in *resurrection*: "And hath raised us up together and made us sit together in heavenly places in Christ Jesus" (Eph. 2:26).

Believers are one with Christ *in His acceptance before Jehovah God*: ". . . He hath made us accepted in the Beloved" (Eph. 2:6).

Believers are *one with Jesus in God*: "For ye are dead, and your life is hid with Christ in God" (Col. 3:3). We are born into the family of God, our names are recorded in the Lamb's book of life. We are seated in the heavenlies with Jesus, we are hid WITH CHRIST in God.

Believers *will be one with Christ in His glorious appearing*: "Looking for that blessed hope, and the glorious appearing of the great God and our Saviour Jesus Christ" (Tit. 2:13). *"When Christ, who is our life, shall appear, then shall ye also appear with Him in glory"* (Col. 3:4). Jesus is coming FOR His saints, and Jude tells us that He will then come WITH His saints: ". . . Behold, the Lord cometh with ten thousands of His saints, to execute judgment upon all, and to convince all that are ungodly among them of all their ungodly deeds which they have ungodly committed, and of all their hard speeches which ungodly sinners have spoken against Him" (Jude 15, 15).

Believers are *one with Jesus as King*. We will reign with Him; we are heirs of God, joint-heirs with Christ to all that He possesses: 'That ye would walk worthy of God, *who hath called you unto His kingdom and glory"* (I Thess. 2:12). "Blessed and holy is he that hath part in the first resurrection: on such the second death hath no power, but *they shall be priests of God and of Christ, and shall reign with Him a thousand years"* (Rev. 20:6).

Believers are *one with Christ in all things*: "He that spared not His own Son, but delivered Him up for us all, how shall He not with Him also freely give us all things?" (Rom. 8:32).

Last, but by no means least, *believers shall be LIKE Christ*: "Beloved, NOW are we the sons of God, and it doth not yet appear what we shall be: but we know that, when He shall appear, *we shall be like Him*: for we shall see Him as He is" (I John 3: 2).

No wonder Peter said, "Whom having not seen, ye love; in whom, though now ye see Him not, yet believing, ye rejoice with joy unspeakable and full of glory!" (I Pet. 1:8).

Yes, salvation brings joy that words cannot express. It brings peace that is beyond all human understanding. I declare with Paul, " . . . *I KNOW WHOM I HAVE BELIEVED, and am persuaded that He is able to keep that which I have committed unto Him against that day!"* (II Tim. 1:12).

Believers are saved NOW. Our sins are forgiven NOW. We are justified NOW. We are sanctified NOW. We are kept by the power of God NOW. We are preserved in the grace of God NOW. We are complete in Jesus NOW. Our names are recorded in the Lamb's book of life NOW. We have been baptized into the body of Christ and are IN HIM—NOW. We are one with Jesus, one in the New Testament Church, NOW. We are just as sure for heaven as Jesus is in heaven, because He is the head of the Church and we are members of His body—flesh of His flesh, bone of His bones.

Are you saved? If you are not, won't you bow your head this moment, and in your own words confess to God that you are a sinner, that you stand in need of sal-

74

vation, and then invite Jesus into your heart? God's unalterable Word promises: *"Believe on the Lord Jesus Christ, and thou shalt be saved"* (Acts 16:31).

The Believer's Hope

THE BELIEVER'S HOPE

"For when God made promise to Abraham, because He could swear by no greater, He sware by Himself, Saying, Surely blessing I will bless thee, and multiplying I will multiply thee. And so, after he had patiently endured, he obtained the promise. For men verily swear by the greater: and an oath for confirmation is to them an end of all strife. Wherein God, willing more abundantly to shew unto the heirs of promise the immutability of His counsel, confirmed it by an oath: That by two immutable things, in which it was impossible, for God to lie, we might have a strong consolation, who have fled for refuge to lay hold upon the hope set before us: Which hope we have as an anchor of the soul, both sure and stedfast, and which entereth into that within the veil; whither the forerunner is for us entered, even Jesus, made an high priest for ever after the order of Melchisedec" (Heb. 6:13-20).

BELIEVERS HAVE HOPE NOW

"Which hope we HAVE . . . ." We are not looking forward to the day when we WILL HAVE hope; we have hope now, and this hope is in One who cannot lie. God made promises to Abraham, and because God could swear by no greater, *"He sware by Himself . . . that by two immutable things in which it was impossible for God to lie. we might have a strong consolation,* who have fled for refuge to lay hold upon the hope set before us."

Our consolation is strong because we hope in the mighty God—the everlasting Father who cannot lie, who cannot break a promise, and who cannot die. Believers "lay hold upon the hope set before us"—and what IS the hope set before us? The hope now possessed by believers is the *assurance* that we will be *with* Christ, we will be *like* Christ, we will have *the mind of Christ,* a *body like* Christ, we will share *with Christ* as joint - heirs of God, and we will reign with Him:

"Blessed and holy is he that hath part in the first resurrection: on such the second death hath no power, but they shall be priests of God and of Christ, and shall reign with Him a thousand years" (Rev. 20:6).

The believer's hope is an "anchor of the soul." I am sure that each of us knows what an anchor is and what it is used for. When a ship "drops anchor" in a harbor, the anchor holds the ship and keeps it from drifting and the winds cannot drive it on the rocks. Believers can say, "Hallelujah for the anchor of the soul!"

I am so glad that God did not save me, put me on board the salvation ship—and then say to me, "I hope you make it into the Haven of Rest. I hope you do not run into any storms, and that you will not be driven on the rocks." God saves us and puts us on board the salvation ship with our wonderful anchor, Jesus Christ. I am not worried about being driven on the rocks or torn apart by the tornadoes and hurricanes of hell, because I am anchored to the Rock of Ages!

The believer's anchor is *"both sure and stedfast."* I like that! Our anchor is unmovable and sure. We are anchored to the stone "cut out of the mountain without hands," the stone which the builders disallowed but God made the Chief Cornerstone. We need not worry about the insecurity of our anchor. *It is stedfast.*

". . . *Which entereth into that within the veil."* Jesus left the bosom of the Father to come into this world and lay His life down. He shed His blood for the remission of

80

sin—and then entered into the holiest and presented the blood to God the Father. Now WE enter boldly into the holy of holies by that "new and living way": *"Having therefore, brethren, boldness to enter into the holiest by the blood of Jesus, by a new and living way, which He hath consecrated for us, through the veil, that is to say, His flesh"* (Heb. 10:19, 20).

What a comfort! In these dark days and perilous hours when Satan is forging his last all-out drive against the people of God, how comforting to the soul to know that we have a hope—sure, stedfast, unmovable, a hope that cannot be destroyed. Our hope is none other than the Lord Jesus Christ, and that hope as an anchor for the soul prevents us from drifting into false religions, false doctrines, "isms" and other sidetracks and detours through which the devil would lead us astray. Certainly in such days as these, everyone needs a hope that is an anchor for the soul.

THE BELIEVER'S HOPE IS IN JESUS CHRIST

"Moreover, brethren, I declare unto you the Gospel which I preached unto you, which also ye have received, and wherein ye stand; by which also ye are saved, if ye keep in memory what I preached unto you, unless ye have believed in vain. For I delivered unto you first of all that which I also received, how that Christ died for our sins according to the Scriptures; and that He was buried, and that He rose again the third day according to the Scriptures: and that He was seen of Cephas, then of the twelve: After that, He was seen of above five hundred brethren at once; of whom the greater part remain unto this present, but some are fallen asleep.

"After that, He was seen of James; then of all the apostles. And last of all He was seen of me also, as of one born out of due time. For I am the least of the apostles, that am not meet to be called an apostle, because I persecuted the church of God. But by the grace of God I am what I am: and His grace which was bestowed upon me was not in vain; but I laboured more abundantly than they all: yet not I, but the grace of God which was with me. Therefore whether it were I or they, so we preach, and so ye believed.

"Now if Christ be preached that He rose from the dead, how say some among you that there is no resurrection of the dead? But if there be no resurrection of the dead, then is Christ not risen: And if Christ be not risen, then is our preaching vain, and your faith is also vain. Yea, and we are found false witnesses of God; because we have testified of God that He raised up Christ: whom He raised not up, if so be that the dead rise not. For if the dead rise not, then is not Christ raised: And if Christ be not raised, your faith is vain; ye are yet in your sins. Then they also which are fallen asleep in Christ are perished. If in this life only we have hope in Christ, we are of all men most miserable" (I Cor. 15:1-19).

In these tremendous verses, Paul declares that he delivered first of all that Gospel which he had rceived in his own heart. He preached Jesus Christ—crucified, buried, and risen "according to the Scriptures." He preached Jesus Christ risen from the dead and seen by many—even by five hundred at one time, and then seen by Paul himself "as one born out of due time." He then asks, " . . . If Christ be preached that He rose from the dead, how say some among you that there is no resurrection of the dead?" He climaxes his message by saying, *"If in this life ONLY we have hope in Christ, we are of all men most miserable!"*

Most of us have at least *one friend* on earth in whom we

can confide, to whom we can carry our burdens, and with whom we can talk freely. I am sure that each of us has at least one friend who would share our tears and sorrows, heartaches and disappointments insofar as is humanly possible—but praise God, believers have a Friend who goes beyond this life!

Regardless of how true our friends in the flesh may be, when we come down to die, those friends can go with us no further than the deathbed, and when we depart this life our hand will slip from the hand of our best friend or even our dearest loved one and we will go out alone into eternity to face Almighty God! But the glorious thing about our hope in Christ is that *He has promised to go with us all the way.* He said, "I will never leave thee nor forsake thee." We are more than conquerors through Him. He promised that if we confess Him before men, He will confess us before the heavenly Father. He will stand in our stead before the Father and He will be our guarantee of heaven's glories when we stand before God to receive our just reward.

I praise God that I am saved NOW. I thank God for what Jesus means to me NOW. He has been exceedingly good to me, He has supplied my every need — past and present; and He will supply whatever need the future brings. He supplies physical needs, spiritual needs, and needs for all eternity. He is the believer's all-sufficiency. In Him we live and move and have our being. He is our life, and *"when Christ, who is our life, shall appear, then shall ye also appear with Him in glory"* (Col. 3:4). Thank God for the hope we have IN CHRIST.

Paul said, "My God shall supply all your need according to His riches in glory by Christ Jesus" (Phil. 4:19). Jesus said, "Seek ye first the kingdom of God and His righteousness and all these things shall be added unto you" (Matt. 6:33). We hope in One who is all-sufficient. And not only is He all-sufficient, but He is anxiously awaiting every opportunity to withhold no good thing from them who walk uprightly.

THE BELIEVER'S HOPE IS IN GOD

In the true sense of the word, we cannot separate Father, Son, and Holy Ghost as having to do with our salvation, because each Person in the Godhead has a specific mission and makes a specific contribution to our redemption and eternal life. God the Father loved us, God the Son died for us, and God the Holy Spirit calls us, "borns" us, *and seals us.*

"But we are bound to give thanks alway to God for you, brethren beloved of the Lord, because God hath from the beginning chosen you to salvation through sanctification of the Spirit and belief of the truth: Whereunto He called you by our Gospel, to the obtaining of the glory of our Lord Jesus Christ. Therefore, brethren, stand fast, and hold the traditions which ye have been taught, whether by word or our epistle. Now our Lord Jesus Christ Himself, and God, even our Father, which hath loved us, and hath given us everlasting consolation and good hope through grace, comfort your heart, and stablish you in every good word and work" (II Thess. 2:13-17).

Paul here thanks God for the believers at Thessalonica, and for the fact that they were saved through the Gospel which he preached to them. Then notice these tremendous words: *"Now our Lord Jesus Christ HIMSELF, and God, EVEN OUR FATHER, which hath loved us . . ."*

John 3:16 is often referred to as "the Gospel in a nutshell": For *God so loved the world,* that He gave His only begotten Son, that whosoever believeth in Him should not perish, but have everlasting life!"

In Romans 5: 8 and 11 we read, *"But God commendeth His love toward us,* in that, while we were yet sinners, *Christ died for us* . . . and not only so, but *we also joy in God through our Lord Jesus Christ,* by whom we have now received the atonement."

We joy in God and praise Him because it was He who so loved us; it was God who *commended* His love toward us. *"What shall we then say to these things? If God be for us? He that spared not His own Son, but delivered Him up for us all, how shall He not with Him also freely give us all things? Who shall lay anything to the charge of God's elect? IT IS GOD THAT JUSTIFIETH"* (Rom. 8:31-33).

The believer's hope in God is not for the moment. We possess this hope NOW—but it is ETERNAL: ". . . And hath given us everlasting consolation and good hope through grace" (II Thess. 2:16 b).

The Psalmist cried out, "Lord, thou hast been our dwelling place in all generations. Before the mountains were brought forth, or ever thou hadst formed the earth and the world, even from everlasting to everlasting, thou art God" (Psalm 90: 1, 2).

One day, if Jesus tarries, I will depart this life and my body will return to dust; but I have a hope, a life that will never end because I HAVE BEEN BORN OF GOD—and since God is everlasting, then my LIFE in Him is everlasting, my hope and my consolation are everlasting. The believer's hope does not end with the grave: we have hope beyond this life in Christ, in God, and in the Holy Spirit.

God so loved me that He gave Jesus. Jesus so loved me that He died for me. And when Christ who is my life shall appear, the same Holy Ghost who drew me to Jesus, convicted me of sin and "borned" me into the family of God, the same Spirit who leads me, assures me, and seals me, will also quicken and raise me and I will have a body just like Jesus' glorious body. That is the hope of every believer!

BELIEVERS HAVE A LIVING HOPE

There are many religions which on the surface look inviting and which are referred to as "good religions," but there is only ONE door to heaven. Jesus is that Door; He is our life:

"Blessed be the God and Father of our Lord Jesus Christ, which according to His abundant mercy hath begotten us again unto a lively (living) hope by the resurrection of Jesus Christ from the dead, to an inheritance incorruptible, and undefiled, and that fadeth not away, reserved in heaven for you, who are kept by the power of God through faith unto salvation ready to be revealed in the last time" (I Pet. 1:3-5).

Through the abundant mercy of God the Father, (who so loved us that He sent the Son of His love into the world to pay the sin-debt), we are begotten and born unto a living hope—a hope that is just as the Lord Jesus who sits at the right hand of God the Father to make intercession for us. The hope that lives in our bosom is *by the resurrection of Jesus Christ from the dead*. Because HE lives, WE live; because HE is in our heart we have a living hope now—a hope that pulsates in our bosom in the very life of Jesus Himself in the Person of the Holy Spirit.

IN I Peter we read, "Forasmuch as ye know that ye were not redeemed with corruptible things, as silver and gold, from your vain conversation received by tradition from your fathers; but with the precious blood of Christ, as of a lamb without blemish and without spot: who verily was foreordained before the foundation of the world, but was manifest in these last times for you. Who by Him do believe in God, that raised Him up from the dead, and gave Him glory; THAT YOUR FAITH AND HOPE MIGHT BE IN God" (I Pet. 1:18-21).

Abraham, the father of the faithful, had unusual hope. Paul describes this hope in Romans 4:18-25: "WHO AGAINST HOPE BELIEVED IN HOPE, that he might become the father of many nations; according to that which was spoken, so shall thy seed be. And being not weak in faith, he considered not his own body now dead, when he was about an hundred years old, neither yet the deadness of Sarah's womb: He staggered not at the promise of God through unbelief; but was strong in faith, giving glory to God; And being fully persuaded that, what He had promised He was able also to perform. And therefore it was imputed to him for righteousness. Now it was not written for his sake alone, that it was imputed to him; but for us also, to whom it shall be imputed, if we believe on Him that raised up Jesus our Lord from the dead; Who was delivered for our offences, and was raised again for our justification."

Abraham hoped against hope. He staggered not at the promise of God, even though that promise was seemingly an impossibility. Abraham believed God, and since God made the promise, Abraham could hope, even though humanly speaking there WAS no hope. The same is true in your life and mine. This living hope of ours is not only IN God — it IS God.

BELIEVERS "REJOICE IN HOPE OF THE GLORY OF GOD"

(Romans 5:2).

As we travel this pilgrim journey in these bodies of clay, we suffer; but we can say with Paul, ". . . I reckon that the sufferings of this present time are not worthy to be compared with the glory which shall be revealed in us. For the earnest expectation of the creature waiteth for the manifestation of the sons of God. For the creature was made subject to vanity, not willingly, but by reason of Him who hath subjected the same in hope" (Rom. 8:18-20).

Believers know that all things work together for good to them who love God, and we also know that nothing can happen to the Christian without God's permission. "If God be for us, who can be against us?" We are therefore commanded, "Let love be without dissimulation. Abhor that which is evil; cleave to that which is good. Be kindly affectioned one to another with brotherly love; in honour preferring one another; Not slothful in business; fervent in spirit; serving the Lord; rejoicing in hope; patient in tribulation; continuing instant in prayer" (Rom. 12:9-12).

As Paul brought his letter to the believers at Rome to a close, he spoke words of encouragement and strength: "Now the God of hope fill you will all joy and peace in believing, that ye may abound in hope, through the power of the Holy Ghost" (Rom. 15:13).

God IS our hope, and the only possible way for us to enjoy our spiritual birthright of joy unspeakable and full of glory is to be filled with all joy and peace IN BELIEVING!

This hope that believers possess is promised by one who cannot lie: IN HOPE OF ETERNAL LIFE, WHICH GOD,

WHO CANNOT LIE, promised before the world began" (Tit. 1:2). In this living hope we can rest with unshakeable confidence.

David cried out, *"My hope is in Thee!"* (Psalm 39:7). *"Thou art my hope, O Lord God"* (Psalm 71:5). "Uphold me according unto thy Word, that I may live; and *let me not be ashamed of my hope"* (Psalm 119:116). Jeremiah confessed, *". . . Thou art my hope* in the day of evil" (Jer. 17:17).

Writing to the believers at Philippi, Paul said, "According to my earnest expectation and my HOPE, that in nothing I shall be ashamed, but that with all boldness, as always, so now also Christ shall be magnified in my body, whether it be by life, or by death. For to me to live is Christ, and to die is gain" (Phil. 1:20, 21).

To sum up the Bible truth concerning our hope:

The Lord Jesus IS our hope (I Tim. 1:1).

We are made heirs according to the hope of eternal life (Tit. 3:7).

We rejoice in this hope which will be firm unto the end (Heb. 3:6).

We have full assurance of hope (Heb. 6:11).

In this living hope, we have an anchor that cannot give way or falter (Heb. 6:19).

We are called in one hope (Eph. 4:4), and this hope is in God.

Our hope is a heavenly hope (Col. 1:5).

Hope is the helmet of salvation (I Thess. 5:8).

"Christ in you, the hope of glory" (Col. 1:27).

THE BELIEVER'S HOPE IS A GLADDENING HOPE

I often say in my meetings that an unbeliever has nothing to smile about, nothing to rejoice about, and nothing to look forward to. Is this a fanatical statement? I answer according to the Scripture:

"The wages of sin is death" (Rom. 6:23).

"He that believeth not is condemned already" (John 3:18).

He that believeth not, " . . . the wrath of God abideth on him" (John 3:36).

". . . Every man is tempted when he is drawn away of his own lust, and enticed. Then when lust hath conceived, it bringeth forth sin: and sin, when it is finished, bringeth forth death" (James 1:14, 15).

"Be not deceived; God is not mocked: for whatsoever a man soweth, that shall he also reap. For he that soweth to his flesh shall of the flesh reap corruption . . . " (Gal. 6: 1, 7, 8).

". . . There is but a step between me and death" (I Sam. 20:3).

With these Scriptures before us, I ask, *What does a sinner have to live for? What does the unbeliever have to look forward to?* David declares that the wicked shall be cut down like the grass and that they are "like the chaff which the wind driveth away." Please study Psalm I in its entirety.

There is nothing stable about sin or unrighteousness: "The Lord shall laugh at him: for He seeth that his day is coming. The wicked have drawn out the sword, and have bent their bow, to cast down the poor and needy, and to slay such as be of upright conversation. Their sword shall enter into their own heart, and their bows shall be broken" (Psalm 37:13-15).

By contrast, *BELIEVERS have a hope that gladdens the heart!* We know that all things work together for good to them who love God; we know that Jesus may come at any moment and we will be caught up to meet Him in the clouds in the air. We know that whether we live or die, God is for us—and if God be for us, what matter who may be against us? "A little that a righteous man hath is better than the riches of many wicked" (Psalm 37:16).

David said, "I have been young, and now am old; yet have I not seen the righteous forsaken, nor his seed begging bread" (Psalm 37:25).

In Hebrews 13:5, 6 we read, "Let your conversation be without covetousness; and be content with such things as ye have: for He hath said, I will never leave thee, nor forsake thee. So that we may boldly say, *The Lord is my helper, and I will not fear what man shall do unto me!*"

The believer has put his trust in the finished work of the Lord Jesus Christ, he rests IN the Lord Jesus Christ, he knows beyond a shadow of a doubt that his sins are covered by the blood and his name is written in the Lamb's book of life. He therefore has a gladdening hope, and he can live with a glad heart even in the midst of this world's tears and sorrow, heartaches, disappointments and failures.

THE BELIEVER'S HOPE BRINGS REJOICING

"Therefore being justified by faith, we have peace with God through our Lord Jesus Christ: by whom also we have access by faith into the grace wherein we stand, *and rejoice in hope of the glory of God"* (Rom. 5:1, 2).

I do not believe in fanaticism, I believe that all things should be done "decently and in order" (I Cor. 14:40). But it is impossible to separate Christianity and emotion because *salvation brings rejoicing.*

In Acts chapter 3 we read a very interesting account of the conversion of a man who was miraculously healed of paralysis, having been lame from birth. This man sat "at the gate of the temple which is called Beautiful, to ask alms of them that entered into the temple; who seeing Peter and John about to go into the temple asked an alms. And Peter, fastening his eyes upon him with John, said, Look on us. And he gave heed unto them, expecting to receive something of them.

"Then Peter said, *Silver and gold have I none; but such as I have give I thee*: IN THE NAME OF JESUS CHRIST OF NAZARETH. *rise up and walk.* And he took him by the right hand, and lifted him up: and immediately his feet and ankle bones received strength. And he leaping up stood, and walked, and entered with them into the temple, WALKING, AND LEAPING, AND PRAISING GOD . . . And as the lame man which was healed held Peter and John, all the people ran together unto them in the porch that is called Solomon's, greatly rejoicing" (Acts 3:1-11 in part)

I do not believe in foolishness in worship, I do not advocate holding a barn dance in the house of God; but if the Church could see a few miracles such as the one performed here, I am persuaded to believe that it would be the means of awakening many sleeping saints who are content to remain babes in Christ, sitting in their spiritual cradles and play-pens while the world around them goes to hell! The Church needs to be stirred. Believers need to waken to the realization that we have a hope that should make us rejoice and praise God!

In Acts 16:25-34 we find the record of the conversion of a very wicked man. Paul and Silas had gone into Philippi preaching the glorious Gospel of the grace of God, and under their ministry a very outstanding lady named Lydia was converted. Later, a poor, demented girl was saved. This girl was possessed of an evil spirit, and she was a slave to money-mongers because her soothsaying brought them much gain. Paul commanded the evil spirit to come out of her, and when her masters saw that the girl would no longer be bringing money into their pockets, they caught Paul and Silas, brought them to the magistrates, and incited the people to rise up against them. They were stripped of their clothing, soundly beaten—and thrown into prison where the jailor *"thrust them into the inner prison, and made their feet fast in the stocks"* (Acts 16:24).

These wicked people shut God's men in—but they could not close God out—hallelujah! At midnight, Paul and Silas prayed and sang praises to God, and God answered with an earthquake that shook the very foundations of the prison, opened all the doors, and loosed the bands of every prisoner! The jailer, waking from sleep and supposing the prisoners all had fled, drew his sword and was about to take a short-cut to hell by taking his own life:

"But Paul cried with a loud voice, saying, Do thyself no harm: for we are all here. Then he called for a light, and sprang in, and came trembling, and fell down before Paul and Silas, and brought them out, and said, *Sirs, what must I do to be saved?* And they said, Believe on the Lord Jesus Christ, and thou shalt be saved, and thy house. And they spake unto him the word of the Lord, and to all that were in his house.

"And he took them the same hour of the night, and washed their stripes; and was baptized, he and all his, straightway. And when he had brought them into his house, he set meat before them, and rejoiced, believing in God with all his house" (Acts 16:28-34).

Only a few hours before, this man had been a mean, blood-thirsty, pagan jailer; but now we find him sitting at the table with God's ministers, eating with them and rejoicing—*"believing in God with all his house."* How marvelous is the grace of God!

From the expression on the faces of some church members today as they approach the church on Sunday mornings, one might think that God is dead, heaven is bankrupt, the Lord Jesus Christ has forsaken us and the Holy Spirit has departed from us! I repeat, I do not believe in a "shindig" or a barn dance in God's house, but God's house *should be* the liveliest, happiest place in the community. I am not suggesting that we should walk around laughing and shouting out "Amen!" and "Hallelujah!" all the time—not at all. There are better ways to praise God than by noisemaking. Christians should be a rejoicing people because we have a hope eternal, and we should rejoice in the hope of the glory of God.

Consider for a moment that *we are sons of God NOW,* we possess *divine nature* now, we are *led by the Holy Spirit* now, Jesus is *preparing a home for us* now—and at any moment we may be changed and caught up to meet Him in the clouds in the air. Why should we not rejoice? May God forgive us for being such thankless people!

BELIEVERS SHOULD ABOUND IN HOPE

"Now the God of hope fill you with all joy and peace in believing, *that ye may abound in hope,* through the power of the Holy Ghost" (Rom. 15:13).

God is the source of all hope. Many times in our testimonial meetings we stand up and praise Jesus—and that is as it should be. We thank Jesus—and we should. We should give Him credit for all that we have, all that we are, and all that we enjoy. But we must remember, "In the *beginning . . . GOD!*" It was God who so loved the world and it was God who turned His head while Jesus died on the cross to pay the sin-debt. Therefore I say, *God is the source of hope*—hope *begins* in God. God gave the divine gift of Jesus that through Him we might have the gift of eternal life.

In the Scripture just quoted from Paul's letter to the believers in Rome, he prays that the God of hope will fill them with all joy and peace—not that they might rejoice and advertise their jubilant victory and experience, but *that they might ABOUND in hope through THE POWER OF THE HOLY GHOST.* There is no place in a deep spiritual life for the practice of frivolous, empty emotionalism. I cannot judge, and I do not know the heart of fellow Christians; but I am afraid that where emotionalism is prevalent, too much of it is in the flesh and too little in the Spirit!

If my cup runs over, my neighbor will be *blessed*—not frozen. Sometimes the actions, demonstrations, and shouts of praise given forth by some people chill the hearts of the spiritually-minded, rather than warming them. Christians should be filled with joy and praise to God—but only to HIS glory—never to glorify self nor to advertise superior spirituality on the part of the individual. A believer who is wholly dedicated to God does not need to hang out a sign; the deep spiritual life of that person will be discovered by his life and through service rendered to his Lord.

THE HOPE OF THE BELIEVER IS CHRIST

". . . For I know whom I have believed, and am persuaded that He is able to keep that which I have committed unto Him against that day" (II Tim. 1:12).

Many people misquote this tremendous verse of Scripture. Paul did not say, "I know IN whom I have believed." The devil believes IN Jesus: "Thou believest that there is one God; thou doest well: *the devils also believe, and tremble*" (James 2:19). The devil and his demons know that Jesus is God, God is Jesus—and on every occasion when the demons met Jesus on earth *they recognized Him as the Son of God.*

It is possible to believe with the head and still not believe with the heart. It is good and honorable to believe that Jesus IS, that God IS, and that *the Bible IS the Word of God;* but head-belief will never save us. To believe ON Jesus is to trust Him. *To believe God* is to believe what God has said, and accept His Word without any question whatsoever. Abraham believed God—"and it was imputed unto him for righteousness" (James 2:23). Paul believed God. In his defence before King Agrippa he said, ". . . *I was not disobedient* unto the heavenly vision" (Acts 26:19), and in the Scripture just quoted from Timothy he clearly affirms, *"I know WHOM I have believed."*

Jesus did not come to earth that there might be a Gospel to preach—*He IS the Gospel*: "In the beginning was the Word, and the Word was with God, and the Word was God . . . And the Word was made flesh, and dwelt among us, (and we beheld His glory, the glory as of the only begotten of the Father,) full of grace and truth" (John 1:1 and 14).

Jesus did not come to earth that there might be salvation —*He IS salvation*: "Looking for that blessed hope, and the glorious appearing of the great God and our SAVIOUR, Jesus Christ" (Tit. 2:13). Jesus IS the Saviour. He is the Way, the Truth, the Life, the Bread of Life, the Water of Life, the Door, the Alpha and Omega. In Him is life—and "when Christ, who is our life, shall appear, then shall ye also appear with Him in glory" (Col. 3:4).

The only possible way for anyone to see God is through Jesus. The only way we can *please* God is in Jesus— He is the only one who ever pleased God upon this earth. At the baptism of Jesus, God the Father said, *"This is my beloved Son, in whom I am well pleased"* (Matt. 3:17). Again, on the Mount of Transfiguration He said, *"This is my beloved Son: hear Him"* (Mark 9:7). Just before Jesus went to Calvary, He looked to the Father in prayer and said, "Now is my soul troubled; and what shall I say? Father, save me from this hour: but for this cause came I unto this hour. Father, glorify thy name. *Then came there a voice from heaven,* saying, I have both glorified it, and will glorify it again. *The people therefore, that stood by, and heard it, said that it thundered*: others said, An angel spake to Him" (John 12:27-29).

God is highly pleased with Jesus, and when we are in Christ, God is pleased with US—we are "accepted in the Beloved" (Eph. 1:6). To the Colossians Paul said, "To whom God would make known what is the riches of the glory of this mystery among the Gentiles; which is *Christ in you, the hope of glory* . . . When Christ, *who is our life,* shall appear, then shall ye also appear with Him in glory"

(Col. 1:27: 3:4).

To the Ephesians he said, "For *we are His workmanship*, created in Christ Jesus unto good works, which God hath before ordained that we should walk in them" (Eph. 2:10).

To the Romans he said, "There is therefore now no condemnation to them which are *in Christ Jesus . . .*" (Rom. 8:1).

To the Galatians he said, "I am crucified with Christ: nevertheless I live; yet not I, but *Christ liveth in me:* and the life which I now live in the flesh I live by the faith of the Son of God, who loved me, and gave Himself for me" (Gal. 2:20).

To the Corinthians he said, "Therefore *if any man be in Christ*, he is a new creature; old things are passed away; behold, all things are become new" (II Cor. 5:17).

To the Philippians he said, "For me to live is Christ, and to die is gain" (Phil. 1:21). And then this dear apostle-appointed, anointed, and used of God as possibly no other mortal was ever used, said, "But what things were gain to me, those I counted loss for Christ. Yea doubtless, and *I count all things but loss for the excellency of the knowledge of Christ Jesus my Lord: for whom I have suffered the loss of all things, and do count them but dung, that I may win Christ, and be found IN HIM*, not having mine own righteousness, which is of the law, but that which is through the faith of Christ, the righteousness which is of God by faith" (Phil. 3:7-9).

My dear reader, *Do you possess Jesus?* Are you born again? Do you know beyond the shadow of a doubt that you are saved? If you have redemption, you possess the believer's hope; but if you do not know that you are saved just as surely as you know your heart is beating, I beg you to bow on your knees this very moment and receive Jesus by faith. "Believe on the Lord Jesus Christ, and thou shalt be saved" (Acts 16:31). ". . . As many as received Him, to them gave He power to become the sons of God, even to them that believe on His name (John 1:12). "For whosoever shall call upon the name of the Lord shall be saved" (Rom. 10:13).

The publican prayed, *"God be merciful to me a sinner"* (Luke 18:13). If, from your heart, you will pray those seven words, God WILL BE merciful to you, He will save you— *and you will know it.* If you do not have the assurance of salvation, give your heart to Jesus now, without fail.

The hope of the Christian is in Christ—I Cor. 15:19.

The hope of the Christian is in God—II Thess. 2:16.

The hope of the Christian is sure and stedfast—Heb. 6:19.

The Christian has a living hope—I Pet. 1:3.

The hope of the Christian is a gladdening hope—Prov. 10:28.

The hope of the Christian is a rejoicing hope—Rom. 5:2.

The hope of the Christian is an abounding hope—Rom. 15:13.

and

THE HOPE OF THE CHRISTIAN IS THE LORD JESUS CHRIST!

The Believer's Position

THE BELIEVER'S POSITION

"Blessed be the God and Father of our Lord Jesus Christ, who hath blessed us with all spiritual blessings in heavenly places in Christ . . . to the praise of the glory of His grace, wherein He hath made us accepted in the beloved" (Eph. 1:3, 6).

In the many years I have been preaching the Gospel, I have found that the most difficult task is getting across to the unsaved the fact that Christ is our salvation and apart from Him it is impossible for any man to please God. The Father said, "This is my beloved Son in whom I am well pleased" (Matthew 3:17); and again, "This is my beloved Son, in whom I am well pleased; hear ye Him" (Matt. 17:5).

Christ alone pleased the heavenly Father, fulfilled every jot and tittle of the law and the prophets, finished the work the Father sent Him to do, and glorified God in every detail of His life, His ministry, His death. Jesus consistently testified, "I came — not to do mine own will — but the will of Him who sent me." He prayed, "Father . . . not MY will, but THINE be done!" Jesus satisfied every demand of God's holiness, God's righteousness, and God's eternal purity.

Without holiness no man shall see God. Nothing that defileth shall enter the city of God, nor whatsoever maketh a lie. Nothing abominable or unclean can enter there. It is clearly taught in the Scriptures that God demands perfection, holiness, righteousness, without spot or wrinkle. What God demands, God provides — and only He COULD provide it, for imperfection can produce no better than itself. It was therefore imperative for a perfect God to provide a perfect salvation. Only a righteous God could provide righteousness. Only a holy God could provide holiness.

But man recoils at the very thought that he must fling himself at the feet of Jesus and declare himself hopeless, helpless, strengthless; that he must look up to God in faith, accepting the finished work of Jesus *plus nothing man can do, provide, or give* in his own strength. All the sinner has that God wants is his heart, and when that is given, God creates within the sinner a NEW heart and a new spirit, making the unbeliever a new creation in Christ Jesus when he embraces the finished work of Jesus by faith (II Cor. 5:17).

To Nicodemus, a ruler of the Jews and a master in the religion of Israel, Jesus said, "Ye MUST be born again." Not understanding how an old man could be born again, Nicodemus asked, "How can a man be born when he is old?" Jesus explained, ". . . Except a man be born of water and of the Spirit, he cannot enter into the kingdom of God. That which is born of the flesh is flesh; and that which is born of the Spirit is spirit" (John 3:4-6 in part).

God creates within us a new heart and a new spirit. The flesh is destined to return to dust; God gave it up in the Garden of Eden. He made no provision to repair the flesh, but He will give us a new body in the first resurrection when Jesus comes the second time without sin unto salvation. He will translate the living saints and raise (in bodies glorified) the saints who have fallen asleep in Jesus. We find the whole truth in the statement of Jesus on the cross: "It is finished!" and what God has finished in Christ, no man can add thereto.

There are no greater words, no weightier words, to be found anywhere in the Bible than the words we will study in this message, nor yet so few words that say so much:

". . . *HE HATH MADE US ACCEPTED IN THE BELOVED*" (Eph. 1:6).

God said to Cornelius, ". . . Send men to Joppa, and

call for Simon, whose surname is Peter; who shall tell thee WORDS whereby thou and all thy house shall be saved" (Acts 11:13, 14). Jesus said, "Verily, verily, I say unto you, he that heareth my WORD . . ." (John 4:24 a). "Of His own will begat He us with the WORD of truth . . . Wherefore lay apart all filthiness and superfluity of naughtiness, and receive with meekness the engrafted WORD, which is able to save your souls" (James 1:18 and 21).

We are saved by grace through faith (Eph. 2:8). Faith comes by hearing, and hearing by the WORD OF GOD (Rom. 10:17). We are born again, not of corruptible seed, but of incorruptible, by the WORD OF GOD (I Pet. 1:23).

From these passages we can clearly see that WORDS — not rituals, not ceremonies — make us Christian. So let us study carefully each word in our text.

1. *"HE"* — *our gracious Provider.*

Apart from God, nothing good or worthwhile could ever be ours. "Every good gift and every perfect gift is from above, and cometh down from the Father of lights, with whom is no variableness, neither shadow of turning" (James 1:17).

The Heavenly Father is the provider of every good and perfect gift. It was He who so loved us that He gave His only begotten Son, willingly, that His Son might take a body like unto our body, and in that body of flesh do for us what we could never have done for ourselves. God is the gracious provider of salvation, redemption, life abundant, life eternal.

Our prayers do not provide salvation. Many have prayed who did not enter the city of God at the end of life's journey. Many are praying in hell today. For more than 1900 years the rich man of Luke 16 has prayed for a drop of water to cool his parching tongue. He prayed that someone would be sent to his father's house to warn his brothers not to come to the place of torment where he was. Prayers, as such, will not save us. The only prayer a sinner can pray and hope to be heard is, *"God, be merciful to me, a sinner"* (Luke 18:13).

Works do not save us. God does not accept us because of our works. Salvation is "not of works, lest any man should boast" (Eph. 2:9). "Not by works of righteousness which we have done, but according to His mercy He saved us, by the washing of regeneration, and renewing of the Holy Ghost" (Titus 3:5).

Our efforts to be good and live good lives will not save us. Our holiness and our righteousness add up to no better than filthy rags in the sight of God (Isa. 64:6). We are not saved by what we are nor by what we can be in our own strength. It is not what we promise to do nor how we plan to live. Our good living, our good deeds, our abstaining from sin — yea, though we give our bodies to be burned — *if we have not Jesus*, these things will profit us nothing!

Those of us who are saved are children of God, hid with Christ IN God (Col. 3:3). We are seated in the heavenlies with Christ (Eph. 2:6). Our citizenship is in heaven, from whence we look for the Saviour (Phil. 3:20). We have these glorious blessings because of God, because of His love, because of His willingness to surrender His only begotten Son into the hands of wicked sinners — sinners who were strengthless, ungodly, unholy, enemies of God. Yet "God commendeth His love toward us, in that, while we were yet sinners, Christ died for us" (Rom. 5:8). Therefore, it is HE — not we. It is "Christ in you, the hope of glory" (Col. 1:27)

If Christ is in us, we are complete: "For in Him dwelleth all the fulness of the Godhead bodily. And ye are complete in Him, which is the head of all principality and power: In whom also ye are circumcised with the circumcision made without hands, in putting off the body of the sins of the flesh by the circumcision of Christ: Buried with Him in baptism, wherein also ye are risen with Him through the faith of the operation of God, who hath raised Him from the dead" (Col. 2:9-12). Spiritual blessings — redemption, salvation, the new birth, being *accepted in the Beloved,* begins in "HE."

2. *"HATH" — a precious certainty.*

The Scriptures do not teach that He MAY, or that He will, at some future date, accept us, but we have here a divine certainty which, if accepted by faith, gives the believer an unshakable assurance. We have a present blessed, eternal position in God. *"Hath"* denotes RIGHT NOW, this moment.

The Scriptures teach that God is an eternal Spirit, with no beginning and no ending. God has always been, He always WILL be. God is from everlasting to everlasting: "Lord, thou hast been our dwelling place in all generations. Before the mountains were brought forth, or ever thou hadst formed the earth and the world, even from everlasting to everlasting, *thou art God!"* (Psalm 90:1, 2). God has been as long as God will be. To be sure, I cannot understand it — and I am happy that I cannot; because if I could understand the eternal God, I would be as wise as God is — and I am certainly glad that my God is stronger, greater, and wiser than I!

Only the spiritually uninformed pray, "Lord, *at last* save us in heaven." The Scriptures clearly teach," He that believeth on Him IS NOT condemned: but he that believeth not IS condemned ALREADY, because he hath not believed in the name of the only begotten Son of God" (John 3:18). "He that believeth on the Son HATH everlasting life: and he that believeth not the Son shall not see life;

but the wrath of God abideth on him" (John 3:36). Believers are not condemned. He who believes HAS — not *will have* at the end of this life, but NOW HAS — everlasting life, while the *unbeliever* is this very moment abiding *under the wrath* of God.

"There is therefore NOW no condemnation to them which are in Christ Jesus . . ." (Rom. 8:1). Notice, "there is NOW no condemnation"; not "There WILL BE no condemnation at the end of life's journey," but NOW, this second, there is no condemnation to the believer. The instant a sinner believes on the Lord Jesus Christ and places his faith in the finished work of Jesus, that split second that individual receives *and possesses* eternal life. We HAVE eternal life NOW; God HATH (already) accepted us. He accepts "whosoever" the moment they put their trust in the shed blood of His beloved Son.

When we believe on the Lord Jesus Christ we become possessors of the Holy Spirit (Rom. 8:9, 14, 16; Eph. 4:30). "Whereby are given unto us exceeding great and precious promises: that by these ye might be partakers of the divine nature, having escaped the corruption that is in the world through lust" (II Pet. 1:4).

We are partakers of (we possess) divine nature. Every believer possesses the Holy Spirit, and we have (already) escaped the corruption that is in the world through lust. Just as surely as God is eternal, those of us who are *children* of God possess in our bosom *eternal life*. Just as surely as Christ died and rose again, WE will rise in the first resurrection: "When Christ, who is our life, shall appear, then shall ye also appear with Him in glory" (Col. 3:4).

As stable and steadfast as God's throne, as sure as God's ever-abiding Word, just that sure are we that we have eternal life; and our life is just as sure to continue eternally as is the God who is "from everlasting to ever-lasting." Christianity does not teach that we are becoming Christians gradually, day by day, but "Beloved, NOW are we the sons of God . . ." I John 3:2).

No believer is enjoying his spiritual birthright unless he can truthfully sing from his heart, "Blessed Assurance, Jesus is mine: O what a foretaste of glory divine!" A be-liever will never become a soul winner until he is positively sure that he is saved, *how* he is saved, and what he possesses when he possesses God's salvation.

3. *"MADE"* — *Believers are the product of a wonderful Manufacturer.*

Sinners (*because* of sin) have made God hide His face from us: "Behold, the Lord's hand is not shortened, that it cannot save; neither His ear heavy, that it cannot hear: But *your iniquities have separated between you and your God, and your sins have hid His face from you, that He will not hear*" (Isa. 59:1, 2).

Sin did even more: Sin caused the Lamb of God, the only begotten *Son* of God, to be despised, rejected, a man of sorrows and acquainted with grief. Jesus bore *our* grief, He carried *our* sorrows, He was smitten of God and af-flicted. He was bruised for *our* iniquities. The chastisement of our peace was upon Him, and *with His stripes we are healed*. All we like sheep have gone astray; we have turned every one to his own way, and the Lord laid on Jesus the iniquities of us all.

When Jehovah God placed upon His beloved Son the sins of the whole world, our sins caused God to literally turn His head while Jesus paid the sin-debt and purchased our salvation at the tremendous price of His own blood: "Now from the sixth hour there was darkness over all the land unto the ninth hour. And about the ninth hour Jesus cried with a loud voice, saying . . . My God, my God, why hast thou forsaken me?" (Matt. 27:45, 46). Of necessity, God turned His back while Jesus died. God cannot look upon sin because God is holy; and when Jesus bore *our* sins in His body on the cross, *our* sins caused God to hide His face from His Son as He paid the sin-debt.

The only possible way a holy God could save and bless us was to make Christ to be sin *for us*, that we might be made the righteousness of God in Christ: "For He hath made Him to be sin for us, who knew no sin; that we might be made the righteousness of God in Him" (II Cor. 5:21). God made His sinless Son to be sin for us, that sinners might be made the righteousness of God in Christ. God has made Christ unto us "wisdom, and righteousness, and sanctification, and redemption: That, according as it is written, He that glorieth, let him glory in the Lord" (I Cor. 1:30, 31).

The reason God has made Christ unto us wisdom, righteousness, sanctification and redemption is *that no flesh should glory in His presence!* Do not forget, God gave up flesh in the Garden of Eden, and what God gives up, it is useless for man to attempt to repair.

Paul cried out, "For I know that in me (that is, in my flesh,) dwelleth no good thing: for to will is present with me; but how to perform that which is good I find not" (Rom. 7:18). Believers are products of the Divine Builder: *"For we are HIS WORKMANSHIP, CREATED IN CHRIST unto good works, which God hath before ordained that we should walk in them"* (Eph. 2:10).

Paul said, "I am what I am by the grace of God," and if you and I ever amount to anything, it will be because we are God's workmanship and He has made us meet for the Master's use! In Genesis 12:1-3 we read, "Now the Lord had said unto Abram, Get thee out of thy country, and from thy kindred, and from thy father's house, unto a land that *I will shew thee:* And *I will make of thee a great nation,* and *I will bless thee,* and make thy name great; and thou shalt be a blessing: And *I will bless them that bless thee,* and curse him that curseth thee: and in thee shall all families of the earth be blessed."

You will note that God promised no roadmaps or signposts. The Scripture is very clear: He commanded Abraham to get up and get out. He said,

"I will show thee . . .

"I will make thee . . .

"I will bless thee . . .

"I will bless them that bless thee."

God is the giver of every good and perfect gift, and apart from Him we can possess nothing of eternal value. All who are saved are saved because of God's love and God's sacrifice. All who are successful Christians are successful because of God; He has made us what we are, and if we will allow Him, he will make us great in that we will be a blessing to all with whom we come in contact. But God can *bless* us and *make* us only to the extent that we will yield to Him and live a life of faith. To His disciples Jesus said, "I will MAKE you fishers of men."

4. *"US" — we are unworthy recipients.*

Have you ever asked yourself the question, "Why did God love me? Why would He allow Jesus to suffer so much for me?" We who are saved were once poor, hell-deserving sinners, dead in trespasses and sins; "But God, who is rich in mercy, for His great love wherewith He loved us, even when we were dead in sins, *hath quickened us together with Christ . . .*" (Eph. 2:4, 5).

We were rebels, but He has reconciled us unto Himself through the death of His only begotten Son. We who were under the curse — helpless, hopeless, and without strength, He has blessed in His beloved Son. We were once under

111

condemnation, the wrath of God hung heavily over our heads; but He has justified us through the shed blood of the Lamb without spot or blemish. We who were once of the world, IN the world, serving the *divers lusts* of the world, He has taken out of the corruption of the world and put in the grace of God, hid with Christ IN God. Positionally we are now heirs of God, joint heirs with Christ, thereby occupying a child's place in God's great eternal family.

"For when we were yet without strength, in due time Christ died for the ungodly. For scarcely for a righteous man will one die: yet peradventure for a good man some would even dare to die. But God commendeth His love toward us, in that, while we were yet sinners, Christ died for us. Much more then, being now justified by His blood, we shall be saved from wrath through Him. For if when we were enemies, we were reconciled to God by the death of His Son, much more, being reconciled, we shall be saved by His life. And not only so, but we also joy in God through our Lord Jesus Christ, by whom we have now received the atonement" (Rom. 5:6-11).

We were sinners, without strength; helpless, and enemies of God when Christ loved us and died for us. Therefore, those of us whom God has accepted on the merit of the shed blood of Jesus are no longer enemies of God, for through the death of His dear Son we are reconciled to God and "we shall be saved by His life." This acceptance is for *whosoever will:* "ALL we like sheep have gone astray: we have turned every one to his own way; and the Lord hath laid on Him the iniquity of us ALL" (Isa. 53:6). All men are in the same category — helpless, hopeless, hell-bound sinners; but through the shed blood of Jesus, God has made us fit to be "accepted in the Beloved."

5. *"ACCEPTED"* — *a glorious truth revealed.*

The Greek word here translated "accepted" means *to*

be endued with special honor. This word occurs only one other time in the New Testament. When God sent the angel Gabriel to Mary, Gabriel said to her, "Thou are highly favoured," using the same Greek word used here in our text. In other words, Gabriel said to Mary, "Hail! Thou art highly favoured, graciously accepted, much graced; the Lord is with thee!" Other translations read, "endued with grace." Just so, the sinner, hearing the good news of the Gospel, (the message of God's love), the death, burial, and resurrection of Jesus, and embracing the message, becomes "highly favoured, graciously accepted, and much graced" by God on the merit of the shed blood of Jesus Christ.

In Genesis 4:7 we read, "If thou doest well, shalt thou not be accepted? and if thou doest not well, sin lieth at the door . . ." Hebrew scholars tell us that the literal translation of the Hebrew reads, "A sin-offering crouches at the entrance." In other words, *Cain's back yard was full of lambs* — many lambs. Abel had been accepted by God because he came as a sinner, and by faith he offered a more excellent sacrifice than Cain (Heb. 11:4). By bringing a blood offering, Abel confessed to God his need of atonement and by faith laid hold on the gift of God. Abel brought his offering in faith, without which it is utterly impossible to please God (Heb. 11:6).

God refused the offering of Cain simply because it was the product of the earth — earth which God had cursed because of sin. Cain came HIS way, and God said to him, "Why will you not accept MY way? There is a lamb at the door, and if you will come my way, you will be accepted just as quickly as I accepted Abel; but if you refuse to bring the blood sacrifice, then I cannot and will not accept you!"

In coming to God for salvation, first there must be *confession for the need of atonement* on the part of the unbeliever. Secondly, there must be *atonement made possible through an innocent sacrifice* — atonement made possible by another. In the third place, *the unbeliever must exercise faith IN the atonement* made by an innocent substitute. The result then is that the unbeliever is accepted by God when he exercises faith in the shed blood of Jesus (the Lamb of God without spot), and rests wholly in Christ, accepting His finished work.

In the book of Leviticus, (the *Hebrews* of the Old Testament), we have a perfect illustration of this: "And he shall put his hand upon the head of the burnt-offering; and it shall be accepted for him to make atonement for him" (Lev. 1:4). The burnt offering brings before us the Lord Jesus Christ, our Saviour. It brings Christ as the One wholly devoted to do the Father's will — the One in whom God the Father is delighted and well pleased, the One in whom He was completely satisfied and perfectly glorified. To the Father, Jesus said just before He died, "I have finished the work which thou gavest me to do." And from the cross He proclaimed, "It is finished! (It is accomplished.) Father, into thy hands I commend my Spirit!"

In the Old Testament era, the Israelite who brought the offering and laid his hand upon it, thus identified himself with it and was accepted. In a far *higher* sense, we who trust in the finished work of the Lord Jesus are accepted by God, putting our faith in the worthiness of what Christ is to God the Father.

Very few believers have ever really discovered this truth: "IN BURNT-OFFERINGS AND SACRIFICES FOR SIN THOU HAST HAD NO PLEASURE. Then said I, Lo, I come (in the volume of the book it is written of me,) to do thy will, O God. Above when He said, Sacrifice and offering and burnt-offerings and offering for sin thou

114

wouldest not, NEITHER HADST PLEASURE THERE-IN; which are offered by the law; Then said He, Lo, I come to do thy will, O God. He taketh away the first, that He may *establish the second*" (Heb. 10:6-9).

God found no pleasure in any sacrifice offered from Eden to Calvary. He *passed over* sin, but these offerings *did not take away sin* (Heb. 10:4). When the priest of God offered the blood — first for his own sins and then for the sins of the people — God passed over the sinner: "When I see the blood I will pass over you" (Exodus 12:13). But had not the sinless Son of God died on the cross, all the blood offered in the Old Testament era would have been to no avail because each sacrifice — lamb, dove, or whatever it was — pointed to Calvary where the Lamb of God would offer ONE sacrifice — once, for all, forever, never to be repeated:

"But this man, after He had offered one sacrifice for sins for ever, sat down on the right hand of God; from henceforth expecting till His enemies be made His footstool. For by one offering He hath perfected for ever them that are sanctified" (Heb. 10:12-14).

The unbeliever is accepted by God only on the merit of the shed blood of Jesus Christ, and without shedding of blood there is no remission, no atonement, no redemption. God accepts us and saves us for Christ's sake (Eph. 4:32). Had it not been for the shed blood of Jesus on Calvary's cross, you and I would be destined to be damned! We deserve hell — and God has a perfect right to send every one of us there; but instead, He laid on Jesus the iniquity of us all (Isa. 53:6; I Pet. 2:24).

The moment we come to Jesus, confessing our sin, acknowledging the need of atonement, calling on God in Jesus' name to save us, HE SAVES US! Because of the death, burial, and resurrection of Jesus Christ, because of our acceptance of the shed blood and His finished work, we are highly favored, graciously accepted, and much graced by God Almighty! It pleases God to save sinners who will come to Him by Jesus Christ.

It pleases God to give us all good things, and to withhold no good thing from them who will walk uprightly, being true bondslaves of Jesus Christ, eating, drinking, and doing whatsoever we do to the glory of God. Such a person will be blessed abundantly of God because of the finished work of His Son in whom we have put our trust for salvation, and to whom we have yielded soul, spirit, and body to be used whensoever, wheresoever, and in whatsoever way will bring glory to Him.

6. *"IN THE BELOVED"* — *a secure position and an undeniable fact.*

Those of us who have been born again through faith in the shed blood and the finished work of the Lord Jesus Christ enjoy God's love to the same extent that God loves His Son. This is the advantage of being "accepted in the Beloved." God loves US with the same love wherewith He loves *Jesus.* All true believers are in Christ Jesus; therefore, "If any man be in Christ, he is a new creature: old things are passed away, behold, all things are become new" (II Cor. 5:17). "To whom God would make known what is the riches of the glory of this mystery among the Gentiles; which is *Christ in you,* the hope of glory" (Col. 1:27). "For ye are dead, and your life is *hid with Christ in God"* (Col. 3:3).

God saves hell-deserving sinners for the sake of His only begotten Son, the Son of His love, the Son in whom the Father has much pleasure: "And be ye kind one to another, tenderhearted, forgiving one another, EVEN AS GOD FOR CHRIST'S SAKE HATH FORGIVEN YOU" (Eph. 4:32).

To the praise of His grace, God has dealt graciously with US — *"in the Beloved."* He has not dealt with us according to that which WE deserve — *but as Christ deserves!* He has not dealt with us according to the *law* — but *according to the riches of His grace!* He has not dealt with us according to justice — but *according to His own loving purpose!* God has not dealt with us as a rich man giving out charity — but *as His equals.* He has not dealt with us just in pity, but plenteously, withholding no good thing, giving us heaven's best, not grudgingly nor of necessity — but graciously, out of a heart of love; not as man gives, but as only God could give — BUT ONLY "IN THE BELOVED."

Unlovely we were, stones in the rough, in the rockpile of sin; but He has made us precious stones, and "hath builded us together" in Christ, He being the chief cornerstone. We were beggars, begging for crumbs along the roadside of the world — but He has set us among kings! We sit together in heavenly places in Christ Jesus (Eph. 2:6). We were slaves to Satan and to sin — but God has translated us into the kingdom of His dear Son, making us heirs, and joint heirs with Christ. We were brands for the burning — but now we are branches connected to the true vine (John 15:5). We were poor, but in Christ we are made rich. God has favored us BECAUSE of Christ, He loved us for Christ's sake. He has favored us because of the finished work of His Beloved Son.

In Christ we are accepted into the Church of the living God — the Church beloved. Christ is our Head (Eph. 5:25 ff), He is our beloved, and we are enriched by the bestowment of His blessings; but these blessings are found only IN the Beloved.

Jesus was the Bread of Life — and yet while here on earth He knew hunger. Why was the Bread of Life hungry?

That He might feed the hungry WITH the bread of life!

Jesus was the Water of Life — yet while He was here on earth He knew what it meant to be thirsty. Why was the Water of Life thirsty? That WE might be invited to drink freely OF the Water of Life.

Jesus was Rest — but while here on earth He was weary, tired, and worn. Why? That He might give US rest.

Jesus was the Prince of Peace — but many times here on earth He was troubled. He passed through dark, troubled hours that WE might have "the peace that passeth understanding."

Man was created in the image of God, and none but Jesus (God's image, the Beloved of God,) could make man again as God desired him to be. Jesus was God in flesh (II Cor. 5:19) ; He possessed the wisdom of God and the power of God. None but Jesus, the virgin-born SON of God, could make US sons. None but the Prince of Peace could bring the GOD of Peace and the *peace of God* to poor, undeserving sinners.

The blessings of God bestowed upon man are always free and full. In the beginning of man's sojourn upon this earth, God placed Adam and Eve in the Garden of Eden — the most beautiful spot this earth has ever known — and commanded them to eat freely of every tree of the Garden except the tree of the knowledge of good and evil (Gen. 1:16, 17).

Adam and Eve abused God's goodness, they were driven from the Garden, and because of their disobedience the whole creation was cursed. But in the midst of this dark hour, God promised the Deliverer (Gen. 3:15) ; and in the fullness of time, *Jesus came* (Gal. 4:4). NOW, since Christ died on the cross (according to the Scriptures), was buried (according to the Scriptures), and is risen (according to the Scriptures), God freely gives to every thirsty soul the

118

Water of the fountain of life. The invitation is free and full: *"Whosoever will,* let him take of the water of life freely."

When one takes of the water of life freely, that one is justified freely by God's grace, through the redemption that is in Christ Jesus (Rom. 3:24). When a sinner believes on the Lord Jesus Christ, God deals with that sinner according to His own loving purpose and worthiness in Jesus the Son. Since this is true, may we not ask with the Apostle Paul, "He that spared not His own Son, but delivered Him up for us all, how shall He not with Him also freely give us all things?" (Rom. 8:32).

God DOES give us all things freely. He gives us *the Holy Spirit* that we may know and *understand* the things freely given to us of God (I Cor. 2:12). The blessings of God are as free as the air we breathe or the sunshine in which we bask; but all of the marvelous blessings *freely bestowed* upon US by God the Father are the result of the *obedience and sacrifice* of the Son of His love—"THE BELOVED!"

One who has received the gift of God, the Lord Jesus Christ, by faith in His finished work is "endued with grace" — grace to meet every need, regardless of how varied and how many those needs may be. That means that God has given us all things — yea, God's fullness:" . . . Ye are complete in Him" (Col. 2:10). We have God's fullness when we have Christ. We have "peace that passeth all understanding" and *God cannot lie* (Heb. 6:18; Tit. 1:2). We have life because Christ IS our life. He came that we might HAVE life, and have it abundantly. We abide in Him as the branch abides in the vine.

We have the fullness of blessing because the Word promises, "My God shall supply all your need." We delight in Him. We have power because we are *kept* by the power of God. We wait upon Him because He said, "I will never leave thee." We have the fullness of grace because He said, "My grace is sufficient." We have the fullness of God's love because *God IS love,* and Jesus said, *"I and my Father are one."* We are hid with Christ in God. We have the Holy Spirit to teach us (I John 2:27) and therefore we learn of Him. We have the fullness of joy unspeakable and full of glory (I Pet. 1:8). We rejoice in Him. We have unshakable assurance because we know that "if God be for us, who can be against us? He that spared not His own son, but delivered Him up for us all, how shall He not with Him also freely give us all things?

Who shall lay anything to the charge of God's elect? It is God that justifieth. Who is he that condemneth? It is Christ that died, yea rather that is risen again, who is even at the right hand of God, who also maketh intercession for us. Who shall separate us from the love of Christ? Shall tribulation, or distress, or persecution, or famine, or nakedness, or peril, or sword? As it is written, For thy sake we are killed all the day long; we are accounted as sheep for the slaughter. Nay, in all these things we are more than conquerors through Him that loved us. For I am persuaded, that neither death, nor life, nor angels, nor principalities, nor powers, nor things present, nor things to come, nor height, nor depth, nor any other creature, shall be able to separate us from the love of God, which is in Christ Jesus our Lord" (Rom. 8:31-39).

As we sing the praises of God and rejoice with joy unspeakable, knowing that all of our needs are supplied and that God's grace is sufficient for us, God grant that we not forget that all blessings are ours because "HE HATH MADE US ACCEPTED IN THE BELOVED."

In closing, let me plead that every Christian not fully

surrendered may here and now yield soul, spirit, and body to Jesus! Pray this prayer: "Lord, take me, break me; mold me and make me *a vessel meet for the Master's use!*"

Of the unbeliever, I beg that you turn your eyes upon Jesus, and in your own words tell Him you are a sinner and ask Him to save you. God will forgive you for Christ's sake, and He will accept you *"in the Beloved!"*

"Verily, verily, I say unto you, He that heareth my Word, and believeth on Him that sent me, hath everlasting life, and shall not come into condemnation; but is passed from death unto life" (John 5:24).

". . . Believe on the Lord Jesus Christ, and thou shalt be saved, and thy house" (Acts 16:31).

"That if thou shalt confess with thy mouth the Lord Jesus, and shalt believe in thine heart that God hath raised Him from the dead, thou shalt be saved. For with the heart man believeth unto righteousness; and with the mouth confession is made unto salvation" (Rom. 10:9, 10).

"But as many as received Him, to them gave He power to become the sons of God, even to them that believe on His name: Which were born, not of blood, nor of the will of the flesh, nor of the will of man, but of God" (John 1:12, 13).

Believers Are Rich

BELIEVERS ARE RICH

Have you ever heard someone say, "I wish I had been born rich—I wish I had been born into the home of a millionaire"? Perhaps there are those—especially among the young people—who wish they had been the child of a movie star, or that their father were President of the United States. Only unbelievers would make such a statement—and the reason they would say such a thing is because they ARE unbelievers and **they do not know the grace of God.**

"For ye know the grace of our Lord Jesus Christ, that, though He was rich, yet for your sakes He became poor, that ye through His poverty might be rich" (II Cor. 8:9). Many believers are poor in this world's goods. So far as money in the bank is concerned, they do not have it. But personally, I had rather have HOPE in the bank of Heaven than to have a million dollars in the banks of earth WITHOUT hope in the Lord Jesus Christ! "For what is a man profited, if he shall gain the whole world, and lose his own soul? or what shall a man give in exchange for his soul?" (Matt. 16:26).

"As sorrowful, yet alway rejoicing; as poor, yet making many rich; as having nothing, and yet possessing all things" (II Cor. 6:10). Thus Paul describes the believer in his letter to the Corinthian church. A believer is the only person who can smile through tears, rejoice in the midst of tragedy, whistle a song when he has not one penny in his pocket and his cupboard is bare of food; for the believer is rich in grace, and he knows full well that his God is all-sufficient and is very capable of taking care of the Christian under any and all circumstances. So far as the human eye can see, believers may have **nothing**—but in actuality, the believes possesses **"all things."**

Heaven is at the disposal of the born again child of God. David said: ". . . The Lord God is a sun and shield: the Lord will give grace and glory: **no good thing will He withhold from them that walk uprightly**" (Psalm 84:11). This is a promise from our God who cannot lie—and the only condition to be met in order to **know** that heaven is at our disposal is to "walk uprightly"—that is, to be dedicated soul, spirit, and body to the Lord God Almighty. In the words of Jesus, "Seek ye first the kingdom of God, and His righteousness; and all these things shall be added unto you" (Matt. 6:33).

John the Beloved, under inspiration, gives us this promise: "If ye abide in me, and my words abide in you, ye shall ask what ye will, and it shall be done unto you" (John 15:7).

"For ye know the grace of our Lord Jesus Christ, that, though He was rich, yet for your sakes He became poor, that ye through His poverty might be rich" (II Cor. 8:9). Believers are rich because He who was rich became poor that through His poverty we who believe might inherit the riches of heaven. What a joy, what a delight, and how refreshing to the spirit to read in God's infallible Word how we inherit all riches in Christ Jesus!

But so glorious the inheritance, so grave the responsibility. We must remember that we are made rich IN HIM —and only in Him: "Every good gift and every perfect gift is from above, and cometh down from the Father of lights, with whom is no variableness, neither shadow of turning" (James 1: 17). In Him we live and move and have our being. In Him we have the grace of God—and we are what we are by the grace of God. Through the pathway of His humiliation, we share the glory of His exaltation. We sit together in heavenly places in Christ Jesus NOW:

126

"But God, who is rich in mercy, for His great love where-with He loved us, even when we were dead in sins, hath quickened us together with Christ, (by grace ye are saved;) and hath raised us up together, and made us sit together in heavenly places in Christ Jesus: That in the ages to come He might shew the exceeding riches of His grace in His kindness toward us through Christ Jesus" (Eph. 2:4-7). Our citizenship is in heaven, from whence we look for the Saviour.

We are saved by grace through faith—and not of works: "Not by works of righteousness which we have done, but according to His mercy He saved us, by the washing of regeneration, and renewing of the Holy Ghost; which He shed on us abundantly through Jesus Christ our Savious" (Titus 3:5, 6). Such a pathway for us by no means suggests that we can believe on the Lord Jesus Christ for salvation, and then live a selfish, self-centered, willful life. If we share His riches and His glory, then we should be willing to share—at least in some small way—His poverty.

How can we share His poverty? We can leave all to follow Him. We can present our bodies a living sacrifice, holy, acceptable unto God, which is our reasonable service (Rom. 12:1). We can put our hand to the plow and refuse to look back (Luke 9:62). We can lay ourselves and all that we have at His feet:

"Then answered Peter and said unto Him, Behold, we have forsaken all, and followed thee; what shall we have therefore? And Jesus said unto them, Verily I say unto you, That ye which have followed me, in the regeneration when the Son of man shall sit in the throne of His glory, ye also shall sit upon twelve thrones, judging the twelve tribes of Israel. And every one that hath forsaken houses, or brethren, or sisters, or father, or mother, or wife, or children, or lands, for my name's sake, shall receive an hundredfold, and shall inherit everlasting life" (Matt. 19:27-29).

Believers can know the fellowship of His sufferings by being made conformable unto His death: "That I may know Him, and the power of His resurrection, and the fellowship of His sufferings, being made conformable unto His death" (Phil. 3:10)·

We can suffer with Him—yes, we can share in His agony of soul, spirit, and body: "If we suffer, we shall also reign with Him: if we deny Him, He also will deny us" (II Tim. 2:12).

Believers can follow in His steps in His humiliation: "For even hereunto were ye called: because Christ also suffered for us, leaving us an example, that ye should follow in His steps" (I Pet. 2:21).

Believers who are sanctified soul, spirit, and body can suffer the despoiling of our goods for His sake: "For ye had compassion of me in my bonds, and took joyfully the spoiling of your goods, knowing in yourselves that ye have in heaven a better and an enduring substance" (Heb. 10:34).

We can suffer outside the camp with Him, bearing His reproach: "Let us go forth therefore unto Him without the camp, bearing His reproach" (Heb. 13:13).

We may count all things refuse (trash), that we may win Christ: "Yea, doubtless, and I count all things but loss for the excellency of the knowledge of Christ Jesus my Lord: for whom I have suffered the loss of all things, and do count them but dung, that I may win Christ" (Phil. 3:8).

There is a vast difference between **redemption**—and **full surrender.** There is a vast difference between being **born again**—and presenting soul, spirit, and body **unreservedly to God in stewardship.** Moses refused to be called the son of Pharoah's daughter. He could have enjoyed the pleasures and riches of Egypt, which in the eyes of the world would have been a glorious privilege and a tremendous opportunity. But Moses rejected that opportunity, "choosing rather to suffer affliction with the people of God, than to enjoy the pleasures of sin for a season; esteeming the reproach of Christ greater riches than the treasures in Egypt: for he had respect unto the recompence of the reward" (Heb. 11:24-26). Moses saw Him who is invisible!

On the other hand, a young man named Demas forsook Paul in his hour of need and turned aside after things of temporal value, "having loved this present world" (II Tim. 4:10). Demas chose to save his life from the suffering which loyalty to Jesus would have brought upon him— and in so doing, he lost "The crown of righteousness" (II Tim. 4-8).

There is a difference between losing one's reward and losing one's soul. Salvation is entirely apart from works. There is not one work that man can perform in order to save himself or **help** to save himself. The Pharisees asked Jesus, "What shall we do, that we might work the works of God?" Jesus replied, "This is the work of God, that ye believe on Him whom He hath sent" (John 6:28, 29). They, like tens of thousands today, wanted to DO something. They wanted to WORK for their salvation. But Jesus said, "THIS is the work of God, **that ye believe** on ME."

All anyone can do to become a Christian is to believe on the Son of God and trust in His finished work. **Jesus** paid sin's debt; He purchased salvation; He finished the work the heavenly Father sent Him to do; **but He has committed the** spreading of the Gospel to US, and we who are born again should work diligently, untiringly, to His glory; and in stewardship we should be willing to share His poverty.

Believers share spiritual blessings: "Blessed be the God and Father of our Lord Jesus Christ, who hath blessed us with all spiritual blessings in heavenly places in Christ" (Eph. 1:3).

Jesus had no place to lay His head. He had no boat—He borrowed a fisherman's boat (possibly Peter's) from which to preach to the multitude. He had no lunch—He borrowed some loaves and fishes from a little boy and fed five thousand hungry people. The poverty He experienced while here upon this earth was OUR poverty—but through that poverty which He took upon Himself, He has made believers rich. He who was in fact the Son of God in flesh, was looked upon by the multitudes as just a miracle-working man because He was made in all things like His brethren—insofar as human eye could see. But in that tabernacle of flesh dwelt very God. Jesus was God in flesh that we, through Him, might become the sons of God in the Spirit (II Cor. 5:19).

The riches we **now** enjoy day by day, the riches we **will enjoy** throughout the countless ages of eternity, are HIS riches—ours through His grace, ours because He was willing to become our poverty and bear our sins on the cross. Eventually, in all things believers will be made like unto Him.

Believers are rich in temporal blessings: "Therefore let no man glory in men. FOR ALL THINGS ARE YOURS ... And ye are Christ's; and Christ is God's" (I Cor. 3:21, 23).

In these verses, Paul is saying what the psalmist said: "No good thing will He withhold from them that walk uprightly ... At God's right hand are pleasures forevermore!"

The Word of God means what it says: **"ALL things are yours."** Whatever the need of the believer — physical, spiritual, mental, financial, whether for time or for eternity, whether small or great—God wants us to ask HIM to meet those needs, and He will abundantly supply. He wants His children to trust Him and call upon Him; He can supply great things just as easily and quickly as he

130

can supply little things. **ALL things become ours in the Lord Jesus Christ: He makes us rich in possessions.**

In Luke 15:11-32 Jesus gives a parable concerning two boys—the prodigal son and his elder brother. It is a passage familiar to all of us. When the prodigal returned home, his father fell on his neck and kissed him, and held a feast in honor of this son who was dead and had become alive. The elder son was angry, and like Cain, his countenance fell; like Ahab, he was pouting. He said to his father:

"Lo, these many years do I serve thee, neither transgressed I at any time thy commandment: and yet thou never gavest me a kid, that I might make merry with my friends!" The father replied, "Son, thou art ever with me, AND ALL THAT I HAVE IS THINE." (Luke 15:29-31). Study the entire seventeenth chapter of John in connection with this.

In Romans 8:16, 17 Paul says, "The Spirit itself beareth witness with our spirit, that we are the children of God: And if children, then **heirs; heirs of God, and joint-heirs with Christ . . .!**" Can you comprehend those words? Are they not beyond our imagination? "HEIRS of God . . . . JOINT-HEIRS with Christ." The promise is there, made by our God who cannot deny His Word. We are enriched to the position of heirs of the heavenly Father, and as joint-heirs we share alike with Christ. As believers we already have the **"earnest** of our inheritance"; we shall possess our inheritance in the ages to come.

Believers share in the riches of His glory: "And the glory which thou gavest me I have given them; that they may be one, even as we are one" (John 17:22). Such declarations from God's Word overwhelm me. What blessed truth! The Lord Jesus shares His glory with us. Not only will we behold Him, look into His face and kiss the scars in His feet—but **we will inherit His glory and be ONE WITH HIM throughout eternity!**

We all know that the visible Church is not perfect here on earth. Paul said, "Husbands, love your wives, **even as Christ also loved the Church, and gave Himself for it**; that He might sanctify and cleanse it with the washing of water by the Word, that He might present it to Himself a glorious Church, **not having spot, or wrinkle, or any such thing; but that it should be holy AND WITHOUT BLEMISH**" (Eph. 5:25-27).

In the visible Church, even the most spiritual believers fall short of the glory of God; but when the Church is caught up to meet Jesus in the air it will be **a glorious Church**, without spot or wrinkle! and it will stand faultless before God. The Church will stand upon her Lord's right hand, and she will be dressed in the gold of Ophar, she will be clad in white linen, and she will share the glory of the King of kings and Lord of lords.

The believer has riches in Heaven: "Lay not up for yourselves treasures upon earth, where moth and rust doth corrupt, and where thieves break through and steal: but lay up for yourselves treasures in heaven, where neither moth nor rust doth corrupt, and where thieves do not break through nor steal" (Matt. 6:19, 20).

Someone has said, "The tighter we grip this world, the lighter grows our grip on things eternal; and the more firmly we grip things eternal, the more lightly we will cling to the things of this life."

In the passage just quoted from Matthew, Jesus is teaching the much-needed truth that this earth is only a place in which to **prepare to live.** Life is as a vapor—it appears for a little while, and then vanishes away. Life on earth at best is but a span of years; and when one's eyes are focused on the riches of earth, he will be **spiritually poor.** The person whose heart and mind is singled on the wealth of eternity will be rich—not only in eternity, but in this life as well; not rich in earthly possessions, perhaps, but rich in spiritual things, bearing much fruit and thus glorifying the Lord God Almighty. It is a divine fact that no man can serve both God and mammon. If we serve God, we **must** make "things" secondary in our life.

Jesus said, "For where your treasure is, there will your heart be also ... Therefore I say unto you, take no thought for your life, what ye shall eat, or what ye shall drink; nor yet for your body, what ye shall put on. Is not the life more than meat, and the body than raiment? Behold the fowls of the air: for they sow not, neither do they reap, nor gather into barns; yet your heavenly Father feedeth them. Are ye not much better than they? Which of you by taking thought can add one cubit unto his stature? And why take ye thought for raiment? Consider the lilies of the field, how they grow; they toil not, neither do they spin: And yet I say unto you, That even Solomon in all his glory was not arrayed like one of these. Wherefore, if God so clothe the grass of the field, which today is, and tomorrow is cast into the oven, shall he not much more clothe you, O ye of little faith? Therefore take no thought, saying, What shall we eat? or, What shall we drink? or, Wherewithal shall we be clothed? (For after all these things do the Gentiles seek:) for your heavenly Father knoweth that ye have need of all these things. But seek ye first the kingdom of God, and His righteousness; and all these things shall be added unto you. Take therefore no thought for the morrow: for the morrow shall take thought for the things of itself. Sufficient unto the day is the evil thereof" (Matt. 6:21, 25-34).

There has never been a preacher who could **preach** like Jesus, there has never been a teacher who could **teach** like Jesus. Who but Jesus would use illustrations like these? The little sparrows do not plant, they do not till the ground, they do not gather harvests; and yet the Heavenly Father feeds them every one! Jesus shames us by asking, "Are YE not much better than they?" Every little sparrow is rich—but believers are much richer, for when the sparrow dies that is the end of his existence, whereas the believer will live throughout eternity with Jesus.

He reminds us to consider the lilies of the field — "they toil not, neither do they spin." Yet compared with the beauty and the softness of the lily, Solomon with all of the glory and splendor his wealth could buy was never arrayed in such richness as the lily. God even clothes the transient grass of the field. Then Jesus asks, **"Shall He not much more clothe YOU, O ye of little faith?"**

He admonishes us not to fret and worry over planning for things of the body. We are to seek first the kingdom of God, and GOD will supply our earthly needs. Paul reiterates this promise in Philippians 4:19: ". . . **My God shall supply all your need according to His riches in glory by Christ Jesus!"**

May God help us to believe that verse with the same sincerity as we believe John 3:16. If we believe that Jesus is able to save us, then surely we can believe that He is able to feed us, clothe us, and give us the necessities of life. We need to recognize that this earth and the journey through this life are not in order that we may strive for riches, power, and earthly glory. This is the place and the time to **get ready** to live, to prepare for true life beyond the grave in the eternity of eternities with Jesus. God will take care of our needs while we sojourn upon this earth, and the riches of believers are reserved to our credit in heaven.

"Blessed be the God and Father of our Lord Jesus Christ, which according to His abundant mercy hath begotten us again unto a lively (living) hope by the resurrection of Jesus Christ from the dead, **To an inheritance:**

> **incorruptible . . .**
> **undefiled . . .**
> **that fadeth not away . . .**
> **reserved in heaven for you,**

who are kept by the power of God through faith unto salvation ready to be revealed in the last time" (I Pet. 1:3-5).

If the millionaires of earth combined their millions, and if those multimillions were turned into billions and the billions multiplied many times over, **the sum total of that wealth could not purchase a home such as Peter describes here!** Earth does not KNOW a home that is incorruptible, undefiled, never to fade away. Such an inheritance cannot be bought with money. The hands of man cannot construct such a home and the **materials of earth** cannot compose it. But every born again believer has a clear title to such an inheritance **"reserved in Heaven"** for the children of God.

Jesus said to His disciples, "Let not your heart be troubled: ye believe in God, believe also in me. In my Father's house are many mansions: if it were not so, I would have told you. I go to prepare a place for YOU. And if I go and prepare a place for you, I will come again, and receive you unto myself; that where I am, there ye may be also" (John 14:1-3). The place Jesus is preparing for believers is described in Revelation 21:

John the Beloved was exiled to the Isle of Patmos "for the Word of God and for the testimony of Jesus Christ." It was there that he was given "the Revelation of Jesus Christ, which God gave unto him. . ." God showed John a new heaven and a new earth, "for the first heaven and the first earth were passed away." And then John saw "the Holy City, new Jerusalem, coming down from God out of heaven, prepared as a bride adorned for her husband."

This new Jerusalem, the Holy City which John saw coming down out of heaven, is the place Jesus is preparing for us now. This is the dwelling place of the bride, the New Testament Church, and Revelation 21:9-27 describes this dwelling place in detail:

"And there came unto me one of the seven angels which had the seven vials full of the seven last plagues, and talked with me, saying, Come hither, I will shew thee the bride, the Lamb's wife. And he carried me away in the spirit to a great and high mountain, and shewed me that great city, the holy Jerusalem, descending out of heaven from God, having the glory of God: and her light was like unto a stone most precious, even like a jasper stone, clear as crystal; And had a wall great and high, and had twelve gates, and at the gates twelve angels, and names written thereon, which are the names of the twelve tribes of the children of Israel: On the east three gates; on the north three gates; on the south three gates; and on the west three gates. And the wall of the city had twelve foundations, and in them the names of the twelve apostles of the Lamb. And he that talked with me had a golden reed to measure the city, and the gates thereof, and the wall thereof. And the city lieth foursquare, and the length is as large as the breadth: and he measured the city with the reed, twelve thousand furlongs. The length and the breadth and the height of it are equal. And he measured the wall thereof, an hundred and forty and four cubits, according to the measure of a man, that is, of the angel. And the building of the wall of it was of jasper: and the city was pure gold, like unto clear glass. And the foundations of the wall of the city were garnished with all manner of precious stones. The first foundation was jasper; the second, sapphire; the third, a chalcedony; the fourth, an emerald; the fifth, sardonyx; the sixth, sardius; the seventh, chrysolyte; the eighth, beryl; the ninth, a topaz; the tenth, a chryso-

136

prasus; the eleventh, a jacinth; the twelfth, an amethyst. And the twelve gates were twelve pearls; every several gate was of one pearl: and the street of the city was pure gold, as it were transparent glass. And I saw no temple therein: for the Lord God Almighty and the Lamb are the temple of it. And the city had no need of the sun, neither of the moon, to shine in it: for the glory of God did lighten it, and the Lamb is the light thereof. And the nations of them which are saved shall walk in the light of it: and the kings of the earth do bring their glory and honour into it. And the gates of it shall not be shut at all by day: for there shall be no night there. And they shall bring the glory and honour of the nations into it. And there shall in no wise enter into it any thing that defileth, neither whatsoever worketh abomination, or maketh a lie: but they which are written in the Lamb's book of life" (Rev. 21: 9-27).

I readily confess that such description is beyond my comprehension. According to the measurements given here, the Holy City will be foursquare: 1500 miles long, 1500 miles wide, and 1500 miles high. The foundations and the gates are described, and **the street of the city will be pure gold.** The Lord God Almighty will be the temple, and the light of the city will be the face of Jesus. There will be no need of sun, moon, nor stars.

All of the kings of the earth will bring their splendor into the Holy City, and the nations will walk in the light of it. (This refers to the saved nations, who, after the consummation of all things, will occupy the new earth.) The Church will dwell in the New Jerusalem, the Pearly White City — but there is a solemn warning: "There shall in no wise enter into it any thing that defileth" **(Peter said our inheritance is undefiled)** "neither whatsoever worketh abomination, or maketh a lie: but they which are written in the Lamb's book of life."

Not only will believers occupy the Pearly White City, but we will also have access to the new earth:

"And he shewed me a pure river of water of life, clear as crystal, proceeding out of the throne of God and of the Lamb. In the midst of the street of it, and on either side of the river, was there the tree of life, which bare twelve manner of fruits, and yielded her fruit every month: and the leaves of the tree were for the healing of the nations. And there shall be no more curse: but the throne of God and of the Lamb shall be in it; and His servants shall serve Him: And they shall see His face; and His name shall be in their foreheads. And there shall be no night there; and they need no candle, neither light of the sun; for the Lord God giveth them light: and they shall reign for ever and ever. And he said unto me, These saying are faithful and true: and the Lord God of the holy prophets sent His angel to shew unto His servants the things which must shortly be done. Behold, I come quickly: blessed is he that keepeth the sayings of the prophecy of this book" (Rev. 22:1-7).

Read these Scriptures slowly; then read them over again. Note every detail of the description of the Holy City. Add up all of these things and see if you can even begin to realize what a tremendous storehouse of riches and wealth lies ahead for believers.

"It pays to serve Jesus, it pays every day,
It pays every step of the way;
Tho' the pathway to glory may sometimes be drear,
You'll be happy each step of the way!"

Serving Jesus not only pays every step of this life's journey — it pays eternal dividends of riches indescribable, unknowable, beyond man's wildest imagination. There cannot enter into the finite heart and mind the glory, beauty, and wealth of the inheritance that is reserved in Heaven for believers.

Heaven is a prepared place for a prepared people. Some may not understand this — but if a person who enjoys drinking, dancing, filthy language, and the company of unsaved people, should accidentally stumble into the midst of Heaven, that person would still be in hell! Those who enjoy ungodliness and unrighteousness could not enjoy Heaven.

The wicked are sometimes compared with swine. Suppose you put a little pig in the livingroom of your home; he will be miserably unhappy. But take him out of your nice livingroom and put him in a mud-hole — and he will at once recline contentedly in the cool, soft mud, as happy as a pig can be! Why? **Because he has the heart of a pig.** By comparison, those who plan to go to Heaven must **prepare** for Heaven — none will enter there by chance. We must prepare for Heaven by believing on the Lord Jesus Christ and receiving Him by faith as our personal Saviour.

Not only is Heaven a prepared place — but **everything we will need there** is prepared. In Revelation 1:17, John said, **"And when I saw Him, I fell at His feet as dead."** It would be impossible for us to enjoy Heaven in these bodies of flesh, blood, and bone. We must have a new body — a body prepared for the Heaven that is being prepared for us.

Paul tells us in I Corinthians 15:50: "Now this I say, brethren, that flesh and blood cannot inherit the kingdom of God; neither doth corruption inherit incorruption." When Jesus appeared in His resurrection body in Luke 24:39-43, He said to His disciples, "Behold my hands and my feet, that it is I myself: **handle me, and see;** for a spirit hath not **flesh and bones, as ye see me have** ... And while they yet believed not for joy, and wondered, He said unto them, Have ye here any meat? And they gave Him a piece of a broiled fish, and of an honeycomb. And He took it, and did eat before them."

Our glorified bodies will be bodies of flesh and bone. The life of the flesh is in the blood. Jesus shed His blood that we might have life, and His glorified body was bloodless. He mentioned the flesh and the bone — He did not mention the blood. He shed His blood for the remission of sin and presented the blood to the Father in our behalf. When we believe in the shed blood, God saves us for Jesus' sake (Eph. 4:32).

When Jesus comes in the Rapture (I Thess. 4:13-18; I Cor. 15:51-55) the bodies of saints who have died will be raised incorruptible and their spirits will be brought with Jesus from Paradise to reunite with the glorified body that will be given to every believer in the Rapture. Jude speaks of the coming of the Lord: "And Enoch also the seventh from Adam, prophesied of these, saying, Behold, the Lord cometh with ten thousands of His saints" (Jude 14). When a believer dies, the body returns to dust and the spirit returns to God who gave it (Eccl. 12:7).

In the passage just quoted from I Thessalonians, Paul declares that when Jesus comes He will bring with Him those who have died in the Lord. Many times in the New Testament, the Spirit (through holy men) tells us that the second we leave this body, we go to be with Jesus. To be absent from the body is to be present with the Lord (II Cor. 5:8; Phil. 1:21-23). The angels carried Lazarus into Abraham's bosom, and to the penitent thief on the cross, Jesus said, "Today shalt thou be with me in Paradise."

There is no doubt in the mind of a Bible believing Christian that the second we die, the spirit goes to be with Jesus; but we will receive our glorified **bodies** when Jesus comes in the Rapture and the first resurrection.

To the believers at Rome, Paul said, "For I reckon that the sufferings of this present time are not worthy to be compared with the glory which shall be revealed in us. For the earnest expectation of the creature waiteth for the manifestation of the sons of God. For the creature was made subject to vanity, not willingly, but by reason of Him who hath subjected the same in hope. Because the creature itself also shall be delivered from the bondage of corruption into the glorious liberty of the children of God. For we know that the whole creation groaneth and travaileth in pain together until now. And not only they, but ourselves also, which have the first fruits of the Spirit, even we ourselves groan within ourselves, waiting for the adoption, to wit, the redemption of our body" (Rom. 8:18-23). The just shall live by faith, not by sight. We hope in the Lord Jesus, we have faith in God, we have no doubt that He will keep every promise.

Paul points out that **the whole creation** — and that takes in everything and excludes nothing — groans and travails in agony, waiting for that grand and glorious hour when Jesus will come; the dead will be raised, the living saints will be changed, and then as God works out His divine plan, the curse will be lifted from the earth. There will be no more thorns or thistles, no thunder clouds, no storms. The animal kingdom will be delivered and will become as Isaiah describes it in Isaiah chapter 11.

"The wolf also shall dwell with the lamb, and the leopard shall lie down with the kid; and the calf and the young lion and the fatling together; and a little child shall lead them. And the cow and the bear shall feed; their young ones shall lie down together; and the lion shall eat straw like the ox. And the sucking child shall play on the hole of the asp, and the weaned child shall put his hand on the cockatrice' den. They shall not hurt nor destroy in all my holy mountain: for the earth shall be full of the knowledge of the Lord, as the waters cover the sea" (Isa. 11:6-9).

This glorious day will come when Jesus comes to reign. Then there will be peace on earth, good will toward men,

141

and in that day the curse will be lifted from the entire creation.

I readily confess that there are many verses in the New Testament that I do not understand — but I **believe them;** for instance, John 3:16, Romans 8:28, Romans 8:17. Many of the verses we have studied in this message are too wonderful for man's comprehension. The believer will not only be with Jesus throughout eternity and live in the place He is preparing for us, but we shall see Him face to face, we shall see His glory and will share that glory with Him.

With Him and through Him we will inherit all things. We are heirs of God, joint-heirs with Christ, and it is impossible for the finite mind to comprehend the depth and the breadth of this COHEIRSHIP. Our eternal reward will include the very closet fellowship with God the Father. We will be to the Father as the Son whom the Father loves but whom He surrendered to Calvary that we might become sons.

We will inherit all the glories of the all-glorious environment that will be God's new creations of heaven, earth, and the Pearly White City. We will have access to the new earth and to God's house in the third heaven. We will reign with Jesus for one thousand glorious years, we will reside in the New Jerusalem with Him, and we will share the eternal riches of the grace of God in the ages to come. In the heavenlies, God will display the bride of Christ — and WE are that bride!

Have you ever asked the question, **"Why does God want to save us, anyway?"** The answer is in Ephesians 4:32: "And be ye kind one to another, tenderhearted, forgiving one another, even as God **for Christ's sake** hath forgiven you." Gave saves sinners for Christ's sake. We were once dead in trespasses and sins, we walked according to the prince of the power of the air, we had our conversation in the lusts of our flesh, we fulfilled the desires of the flesh and of the mind and we were by nature the children of wrath. "BUT GOD, who is rich in mercy, for His great love wherewith He loved us, even when we were dead in sins, hath quickened us together with Christ..." (Eph. 2:1-6 in part).

"BUT GOD...! ! !" God, who is rich in mercy toward us and who loved us with the great love that only God could have, commended that love toward us in that **"while we were yet sinners, Christ died for us"** (Romans 5:8). Even when we were dead in sins, God permitted Jesus to leave Heaven's glory, come to earth's sorrows, and lay down His life for us that we might, through His death and the shed blood of His cross, be quickened together with Christ.

We are saved by grace through faith. We are God's children on the merit of the finished work of Jesus Christ, the shed blood of His cross. God has "raised us up together, and made us sit together in heavenly places in Christ Jesus: That in the ages to come He might shew the exceeding riches of His grace in His kindness toward us through Christ Jesus" (Eph. 2:6, 7).

Yes, God will display the Church in the Pearly White City, to show to all His creatures the exceeding riches of His grace — and every believer possesses God's grace: **"For the grace of God that bringeth salvation hath appeared to all men"** (Tit. 2:11). There is no such thing as salvation apart from grace. If you are saved, you possess God's grace and the RICHES of His grace — riches past finding out, unknowable riches, beyond man's ability to understand. But in the eternity of eternities God will display the riches of His grace in the believers who make up the New Testament Church and who will abide in the Pearly White City.

Are you saved? If you are **not** saved, can you see what you are missing? Can you see what you are **going to miss** when only those whose names are written in the Lamb's book of life enter this Holy City which John saw descending from God out of Heaven?

If you are not saved, you CAN BE SAVED if you will just bow your head and invite Jesus to come into your heart. He promised to save you the moment you invite Him into your heart and receive Him by faith — and God's promises are sure. He cannot lie.

"For God so loved the world, that He gave His only begotten Son, that whosoever believeth in Him should not perish, but have everlasting life" (John 3:16).

"He that believeth on Him is not condemned: but he that believeth not is condemned already, because he hath not believed in the name of the only begotten Son of God" (John 3:18).

"Verily, verily, I say unto you, He that heareth my word, and believeth on Him that sent me, hath everlasting life, and shall not come into condemnation; but is passed from death unto life" (John 5:24).

"That if thou shalt confess with thy mouth the Lord Jesus, and shalt believe in thine heart that God hath raised Him from the dead, thou shalt be saved. For with the heart man believeth unto righteousness; and with the mouth confession is made unto salvation" (Rom. 10:9, 10).

"For by grace are ye saved through faith; and that not of yourselves: it is the gift of God: Not of works, lest any man should boast" (Eph. 2:8, 9).

"Not by works of righteousness which we have done, but according to His mercy He saved us, by the washing of regeneration, and renewing of the Holy Ghost" (Tit. 3:5).

"Thanks be unto God for His unspeakable gift!" (II Cor. 9:15).

The Believer's Inheritance

THE BELIEVER'S INHERITANCE

"Blessed be the God and Father of our Lord Jesus Christ, who hath blessed us with all spiritual blessings in heavenly places in Christ: According as He hath chosen us in Him before the foundation of the world, that we should be holy and without blame before Him in love: Having predestinated us unto the adoption of children by Jesus Christ to Himself, according to the good pleasure of His will, to the praise of the glory of His grace, wherein He hath made us accepted in the beloved. In whom we have redemption through His blood, the forgiveness of sins, according to the riches of His grace; wherein He hath abounded toward us in all wisdom and prudence; Having made known unto us the mystery of His will, according to His good pleasure which He hath purposed in Himself: That in the dispensation of of the fulness of times He might gather together in one all things in Christ, both which are in heaven, and which are on the earth; even in Him: In whom also we have obtained an inheritance, being predestinated according to the purpose of Him who worketh all things after the counsel of His own will: That we should be to the praise of His glory, who first trusted in Christ. In whom ye also trusted, after that ye heard the word of truth, the Gospel of your salvation: in whom also after that ye believed, ye were sealed with that Holy Spirit of promise, which is the earnest of our inheritance until the redemption of the purchased possession, unto the praise of His glory" (Eph. 1:3-14).

God the Father has not forgotten us in making out His will. We who have put our faith and trust in the shed blood of the Lord Jesus Christ have been remembered in the Father's will and we have an eternal inheritance. Writing to the Romans Paul said, "For as many as are led by the

Spirit of God, they are the sons of God. . . . The Spirit itself beareth witness with our spirit, that we are the children of God: And if children, then heirs of God, and joint-heirs with Christ; if so be that we suffer with Him, that we may be also glorified together" (Rom. 8:14-17 in part).

It is difficult for me to really take in the tremendous truth of this statement. *"And if children, then heirs—heirs of God and joint-heirs with Christ."* God the Father makes every born again believer to be a joint-heir with the only begotten Son. It is too wonderful to understand, but *it IS divine truth.* Therefore we can accept it and rest in it. We have an inheritance. *We are joint-heirs with Jesus.*

THE BIBLE DESCRIBES OUR INHERITANCE

"Blessed be the God and Father of our Lord Jesus Christ, which according to His abundant mercy hath begotten us again unto a lively (living) hope by the resurrection of Jesus Christ from the dead, to an inheritance incorruptible, and undefiled, and that fadeth not away, reserved in heaven for you, who are kept by the power of God through faith unto salvation ready to be revealed in the last time. Wherein ye greatly rejoice, though now for a season, if need be, ye are in heaviness through manifold temptations: That the trial of your faith, being much more precious than of gold that perisheth, though it be tried with fire, might be found unto praise and honour and glory at the appearing of Jesus Christ: Whom having not seen, ye love; in whom, though now ye see Him not, yet believing, ye rejoice with joy unspeakable and full of glory: receiving the end of your faith, even the salvation of your souls" (I Pet. 1:3-9).

From these verses we learn that *our inheritance is IN-CORRUPTIBLE.* I did not receive an earthly inheritance. I was reared in a poor home, and while my father always provided enough food for us to eat, clothes to wear, and a comfortable house in which to live, when he went to be with the Lord he did not leave an inheritance to us. We lived on a very small farm, and it was heavily mortgaged. Although none of the eight children in our family received a tangible inheritance, we have the memory of a dear, kind loving father—and that memory is sweet even though he did not bequeath to us houses and lands, stocks and bonds.

But my heavenly Father—the Father of all believers—is very able, capable, and willing to remember every child of His in His will, and that which He has bequeathed to us is an *inheritance incorruptible.* It will never decay, it will never dissolve nor fade away; it is eternal—and it is protected by Almighty God.

The home in which I now live with my own family has been given to me, and is being paid for month by month through the goodness of God and the liberality of the people who have stood by me during the many years of my evangelistic ministry. My house is fifteen years old, it is still not completely paid for, it is heavily mortgaged—and there has not been one year since it was built that I have not had to spend money on it for upkeep—painting, repairs, insurance, taxes, and many other small items that add up to a considerable outlay of money. I thank God for the house in which I live—but it costs money to keep it up, and in spite of all that I can do it is growing older with every sunrise and sunset. In other words, *it is NOT incorruptible,* it is not *undefiled,* and it is *"fading away."* But my home in heaven will never need painting, it will never need new shingles on the roof—no repairs, no upkeep. It is incorruptible! Hallelujah! What a home!

Our heavenly inheritance is also UNDEFILED. The inheritance of the believer is just as pure, just as clean, as the God who gives it to us on the merit of the finished work of Jesus Christ and our faith in Him as Saviour. We live in a world that is defiled; there is ugliness all around us; but in that home over there which is the inheritance of every believer, there is nothing ugly, there is nothing dirty, there is nothing that will defile. That heavenly home is spotless and without fault.

Our eternal inheritance FADETH NOT AWAY. It will never decay, it will never grow old, it will never be in need of repairs. Jesus said, "In my Father's house are many mansions . . . *I go to prepare a place for YOU.*" This declaration makes it plain that when Jesus made this statement there were ALREADY "many mansions" in the Father's house; but those mansions are not our inheritance; we will not live in them. Whose mansions they are, I do not know. God the Father has a mansion, and what provision He has made for the cherubim, seraphim, and angels we do not know. But Jesus said, "I go to prepare a place for you. And if I go, I will come again, and receive you unto myself; that where I am, there ye may be also" (John 14:1-3 in part).

Jesus is preparing a place for us, and that place is the Pearly White City. (Study Revelation chapter 21.) When the bride is complete, that city will be complete. Jesus is preparing it for believers, members of the New Testament Church by the grace of God through faith in His shed blood. We are one in Christ—one body. We will live in the Pearly White City—a dwelling without spot or wrinkle, without blemish of any kind. It is incorruptible, undefiled, and it will never fade away.

In Revelation 21 John tells of the materials of which the Holy City is constructed—such materials as pure gold, diamonds, rubies; turn to the twenty-first chapter of Revelation and read the description of that city. These materials will not corrupt, they will never be defiled, and they are fadeless.

Our inheritance is RESERVED. It is safe because it is reserved in heaven for us. What an inheritance!!!

Our inheritance is in Christ.

Our inheritance is incorruptible.

Our inheritance is undefiled.

Our inheritance fadeth not away.

Our inheritance is reserved in Heaven. Praise God! We have been remembered in His will!

Our inheritance is rich IN GLORY. Let me point out just a few things to be inherited by believers when we stand before Jesus to receive our rewards at the judgment seat for believers at the marriage supper in the sky:

"For we must all appear before the judgment seat of Christ; that every one may receive the things done in his body, according to that he hath done, whether it be good or bad" (II Cor. 5:10).

"Wherefore I also, after I heard of your faith in the Lord Jesus, and love unto all the saints, cease not to give thanks for you, making mention of you in my prayers; that the God of our Lord Jesus Christ, the Father of glory, may give unto you the spirit of wisdom and revelation in the knowledge of Him: The eyes of your understanding being enlightened; that ye may know what is the hope of His calling, and what the riches of the glory of His inheritance in the saints. And what is the exceeding greatness of His power to us-ward who believe, according to the working of His mighty power, which He wrought in Christ, when He raised Him from the dead, and set Him at His own right hand in the heavenly places, far above all principality, and power, and might, and dominion, and every name that is

151

named, not only in this world, but also in that which is to come" (Eph. 1:15-21).

Paul wanted his fellow-Christians to be free from ignorance and to have knowledge and understanding such as only God can impart. He wanted the eyes of their understanding to be opened that they might know the hope of God's calling and the riches and glory of His inheritance in the saints.

Our inheritance is rich in PORTION: "Preserve me, O God: for in thee do I put my trust ... *The Lord is the POR-TION of mine inheritance* and of my cup: thou maintainest my lot" (Psa. 16:1,5). All that we have, all that we are, all that we will ever be or inherit, is in Jesus Christ. *"And He is before all things, and by Him all things consist"* (Col. 1:17).

Jesus is the HUB of the wheel of salvation and all the spokes of the wheel are connected to the Hub. Apart from Him there could be no life, no peace, no joy, no inheritance. In Him we live, and move, and have our being. And all things are to be done to glorify Him—*whatsoever* we do, we should do it all to the glory of God, and God glories in His Son.

Peter asked Jesus about the apostles' future place in the kingdom, and Jesus answered: "Verily I say unto you, That ye which have followed me, IN THE REGENERATION when the Son of man shall sit in the throne of His glory, ye also shall sit upon twelve thrones, judging the twelve tribes of Israel. And every one that hath forsaken houses, or brethren, or sisters, or father, or mother, or wife, or children, or lands, for my name's sake, SHALL RECEIVE AN HUNDREDFOLD, AND SHALL INHERIT EVER-LASTING LIFE" (Matt. 19:28, 29).

We are the recipients of eternal life NOW because we are regenerated through the power of God when we exercise faith in the finished work of Jesus Christ. We inherit eternal life on the merit of His death, burial, and resurrection, "according to the Scriptures."

Because we are sons of God, having inherited eternal life through Jesus Christ our Lord, we will inherit a body like unto His glorious body. "Behold, what manner of love the Father hath bestowed upon us, that we should be called the sons of God: Therefore the world knoweth us not, because it knew Him not. Beloved, now are we the sons of God, and it doth not yet appear what we shall be: but we know that, when He shall appear, WE SHALL BE LIKE HIM; for we shall see Him as He is. And every man that hath this hope in Him purifieth himself, even as He is pure" (I John 3:1-3).

All believers are sons of God NOW. All believers possess divine nature NOW (II Pet. 1:4). All believers possess the Holy Ghost NOW (Rom. 8:9, 14, 16; Eph. 4:30); and we will inherit a *glorified body* when Jesus comes in the Rapture. To the Corinthian believers Paul said, "For we know that if our earthly house of this tabernacle (our body) were dissolved, we have a building of God, an house not made with hands, eternal in the heavens. For in this we groan, earnestly desiring to be clothed upon with our house which is from heaven . . . For we that are in this tabernacle do groan, being burdened: not for that we would be unclothed, but clothed upon, that mortality might be swallowed up of life . . . Therefore we are always confident, knowing that, whilst we are at home in the body, we are absent from the Lord: (For we walk by faith, not by sight:) We are confident, I say, and willing rather to be absent from the body, and to be present with the Lord" (II Cor. 5:1-8 in part). Paul believed and preached that the very moment a Christian departs this life, the spirit goes to be with the Lord.

Again Paul said, "For I am in a strait betwixt two, having a desire to depart, and to be with Christ; which is far better: Nevertheless to abide in the flesh is more needful for you" (Phil. 1:23, 24). Paul wanted to depart the flesh and be with Christ — which for him would have been far better; but for the sake of the believers at Philippi it was better that he remain in the flesh, abide with them, and minister to them.

The Bible does not teach "soul-sleep." There is much misunderstanding among believers concerning what happens when a Christian dies. The split second a believer departs this life, the spirit goes to be with the Lord; but the believer does not inherit his glorified body at that time. That will be given to him in the first resurrection.

John the beloved tells us, "And I heard a voice from heaven saying unto me, Write, Blessed are the dead which die in the Lord from henceforth: Yea, saith the Spirit, THAT THEY MAY REST FROM THEIR LABOURS; and their works do follow them"! (Rev. 14:13). When a believer leaves this life he goes to be with the Lord, but he does not have his glorified body. He is conscious, he rejoices, he knows what is going on in heaven and I personally believe he knows much of what is going on here on earth. He does not see or know things that would make him sad, because there are no tears in heaven.

There are godly mothers who pray many years for a son or a daughter, yet depart this life to be with Jesus before that loved one is saved. Later, when that son or daughter is born again, I believe that somehow that dear mother knows it. Luke 15:10 tells us that there is joy in the presence of the angels over one sinner who repents. It does not say that the *angels* are joyful, but that there is joy *in the presence* of the angels. Certainly, someone could rejoice in my pres-

154

ence and I would not necessarily be rejoicing with that one. The only person who could rejoice over the salvation of a sinner would be a saint in Paradise, or Jesus who died for sinners. Angels know nothing of the joy salvation brings. "I say unto you, that likewise joy shall be in heaven over one sinner that repenteth, more than over ninety and nine just persons, which need no repentance . . . Likewise, I say unto you, there is joy in the presence of the angels of God over one sinner that repenteth" (Luke 15:7 and 10).

Paul clearly tells us when we will receive our glorified body: "But now is Christ risen from the dead, and become the firstfruits of them that slept. For since by man came death, by man came also the resurrection of the dead. For as in Adam all die, even so in Christ shall all be made alive. But every man in his own order: Christ the firstfruits; *afterward, they that are Christ's at His coming*" (I Cor. 15:20-23).

Christ is the firstfruits; He is our life; He is the resurrection AND the life, and because HE lives, WE live. "Behold, I shew you a mystery: We shall not all sleep (die), but we shall all be *changed*. In a moment, in the twinkling of an eye, at the last trump: for the trumpet shall sound, and the dead shall be raised incorruptible, and we shall be changed. *For this corruption must put on incorruption, and this mortal must put on immortality*" (I Cor. 15:51-53).

This mortal must put on immortality. This body of death must be changed; "Now this I say, brethren, *that flesh and blood cannot inherit the kingdom of God; neither doth corruption inherit incorruption*" (I Cor. 15:50). Christ is the firstfruits, and we who are His because of our faith in His shed blood will inherit a body exactly like His glorious resurrection body. In the twenty-fourth chapter of Luke we read of the ministry of the risen Christ.

Writing to the Colossians Paul said, "When Christ, who is our life, shall appear, then shall ye also appear with Him in glory" (Col. 3:4). When we appear with Jesus in glory, we will appear in a body like unto His resurrection body. We will *inherit* that body when the Church is raptured and those who have died in Christ are raised incorruptible. Study I Thessalonians 4:13-18.

The Scripture does not tell us what kind of bodies believers have who are now resting in Paradise. They are not unconscious, and they do have some form of body. When Jesus was transfigured (as recorded in Matthew 17:1-3 and Luke 9:27-36), Moses and Elijah came down and talked with Him. Peter and the other disciples recognized Moses and Elijah, yet these two men had been dead for many years. They appeared in a body, the form of which we do not know and about which we need not speculate; but we do know that they were *recognizable.* I personally believe that the saints in heaven today have a body similar to that of Jesus when He said to Mary, "Touch me not; for I am not yet ascended to my Father: but go to my brethren, and say unto them, I ascend unto my Father, and to your Father; and to my God, and your God" (John 20:17).

In Matthew 28:9 we read, " . . . Jesus met them, saying, All hail. And *they came and held Him by the feet,* and worshipped Him." Some have suggested that there is a contradiction of Scripture between this and John 20:17; but not so. When Jesus spoke to Mary in the garden, He spoke as the High Priest of God fulfilling the day of atonement (study Leviticus 16). He had accomplished the sacrifice, the Lamb had been slain, the blood had been poured out; and He was then on His way to present His blood to the Father in heaven. *Between* His meeting with Mary in the garden and His meeting with the disciples as recorded in

Matthew 28:9, He ascended to the Father, presented the blood, and returned in His glorified body.

I personally believe that the saints who are resting from their labors awaiting the first resurrection, have bodies like the body Jesus had during those moments between the time He walked from the tomb until the time He went to the Father and returned to earth in the body He had while He remained here upon earth for forty days — the body upon which the disciples gazed as He ascended into the clouds as recorded in Acts 1:8-10. It thrills my soul to know that one day I will inherit a body just like the body of Jesus! No more pain, no more tears, no more sorrow and disappointment, no mort sickness, no more death! Hallelujah! But there is more:

We are now *accepted in the Beloved* (Eph. 1:6).

We are *sons of God NOW* (I John 3:2).

We are *sealed by the Holy Spirit NOW* (Eph. 4:30).

Positionally, we are raised with Jesus, and we *sit with Him in heavenly places NOW* (Eph. 2:6).

The moment we receive Jesus, *we receive everything He did for us* — in His life, in His death, burial, and resurrection. Paul said, "I am crucified with Christ: nevertheless I live; yet not I, but Christ liveth in me: and the life which I now live in the flesh I live by the faith of the Son of God, who loved me, and gave Himself for me" (Gal. 2:20).

God has made us *to sit together with Christ*. Before we were saved, we sat with the enemies of Jesus, in darkness and in sin. We walked in the counsel of the ungodly. We stood with sinners. We were by nature the children of wrath. But NOW, having believed from the heart unto salvation, we have been translated out of darkness into light, and we sit together with Christ in heavenly places. One day we will literally sit with Him in the Pearly White City.

WE WILL INHERIT THE POSITION OF KINGS

". . . Unto Him that loved us, and washed us from our sins in His own blood, and hath made us kings and priests unto God and His Father; to Him be glory and dominion for ever and ever. Amen" (Rev. 1:5 b, 6).

God the Father has not only redeemed us and given us eternal life; He has also promoted us and we will reign with Jesus as kings over the earth when He comes in the revelation with His saints as described in Revelation 19:11-15. We will reign as kings with Jesus for one thousand glorious years on this earth during the Millennium.

There are those who spiritualize the kingdom on earth and the reign with Jesus as king; but it is a literal kingdom. Jesus will sit on the throne of David (Luke 1:32, 33). The temple will be rebuilt (Acts 15:16). And believers will reign with Christ right here on this earth: "And when He had taken the book, the four beasts and four and twenty elders fell down before the Lamb, having every one of them harps, and golden vials full of odours, which are the prayers of saints. And they sung a new song, saying, Thou art worthy to take the book, and to open the seals thereof: for thou wast slain, and hast redeemed us to God by thy blood out of every kindred, and tongue, and people, and nation; And hast made us unto our God kings and priests: and we shall reign on the earth" (Rev. 5:8-10).

I see no reason for misunderstanding here. We are the Church, we have been redeemed out of every blood, kindred, tongue, and nation of earth. We are made kings and priests, *and we shall reign on the earth.*

"Blessed are the meek: *for they shall inherit the earth*" (Matt. 5:5).

"But the meek shall inherit the earth; and shall delight themselves in the abundance of peace" (Psa. 37:11).

158

"The righteous shall inherit the land, and dwell therein forever" (Psa. 37:29).

To reign on this earth with Jesus is our future inheritance. Positionally we are kings and priests now. Positionally we sit with Jesus in heaven now. Positionally we sit with Christ in God NOW. We are sons of God now. But when Jesus comes for the Church and the saints who have died in the Lord are raised incorruptible, living saints will be changed in the twinkling of an eye. We will rejoice at the marriage supper in the sky, we will receive our reward, and we will return with Christ to reign on earth.

"IF WE SUFFER, WE SHALL ALSO REIGN WITH HIM: IF WE DENY HIM, He also will deny us" (II Tim. 2:12). According to God's infallible Word, we will reign with Jesus right here on earth. But our inheritance goes even further than that:

"And he shewed me a pure river of water of life, clear as crystal, proceeding out of the throne of God and of the Lamb. In the midst of the street of it, and on either side of the river, was there the tree of life, which bare twelve manner of fruits, and yielded **her** fruit every month: and the leaves of the tree were for the healing of the nations. And there shall be no more curse: but the throne of God and of the Lamb shall be in it; and His servants shall serve Him: And they shall see His face; and His name shall be in their foreheads. And there shall be no night there; and they need no candle, neither light of the sun; for the Lord God giveth them light: *and they shall reign for ever and ever.* And he said unto me, These sayings are faithful and true: and the Lord God of the holy prophets sent His angel to shew unto His servants the things which must shortly be done. Behold, I come quickly: blessed is he that keepeth the sayings of the prophecy of this book" (Rev. 22:1-7).

159

We who are born again will reign with Jesus forever and ever. And "of the increase of His government and peace there shall be no end" (Isa. 9:7 a).

". . . And, behold, thou shalt conceive in thy womb, and bring forth a son, and shalt call His name JESUS. He shall be great, and shall be called the Son of the Highest: and the Lord God shall give unto Him the throne of His father David: And He shall reign over the house of Jacob for ever; and of His kingdom there shall be no end" (Luke 1:31-33).

THE BIBLE BLUEPRINT OF THINGS AHEAD

"And after they had held their peace, James answered, saying, Men and brethren, hearken unto me: Simeon hath declared how God at the first did visit the Gentiles, to take out of them a people for His name." (This has been going on for more than 1900 years. We are in that period now. The Holy Ghost is calling out a Gentile bride — the Church.) "And to this agree the words of the prophets; as it is written, After this (after the completion of the Church and after the Rapture) I will return, and will build again the tabernacle of David, which is fallen down; and I will build again the ruins thereof, and I will set it up: That the residue of men might seek after the Lord, and all the Gentiles, upon whom my name is called, saith the Lord, who doeth all these things. *Known unto God are all His works from the beginning of the world"* (Acts 15:13-18).

To me, this is the clearest outline of God's plan of the ages in all the Word of God. We know that since Pentecost God has been calling out a people—all who will believe on Jesus. The Holy Spirit came on the Day of Pentecost to testify of Jesus; He draws men TO Jesus, convicts them of sin — and through His power "borns" them into God's family. He indwells us, leads us, assures us and seals us;

160

and He will go out of the world with the Church at the time of the Rapture.

Jesus WILL return to this earth, the tabernacle WILL be rebuilt in Jerusalem, Jesus will sit on the throne of David in that city and reign over the earth — and we will reign with Him. That is included in our inheritance. Hallelujah!

THE CAPSTONE OF THE GREAT PYRAMID OF OUR INHERITANCE

"He that overcometh shall inherit all things; and I will be his God, and he shall be my son" (Rev. 21:7).

"The Lord knoweth the days of the upright: and their inheritance shall be for ever" (Psalm 37:18).

If I had a thousand hands I would raise them all for Jesus. If I had a thousand tongues I would use them all to say, "Thank God for Jesus!" I shall never cease to praise God for saving my soul, and I shall never cease to praise Him for His holy Word which enlightens and instructs me concerning what believers possess in Jesus NOW and what we will inherit in the life to come. I am so thankful — and I praise God from the depths of my soul — that I know beyond a shadow of doubt that I am saved and covered by the blood!

I know that all I am, all that I have and enjoy, and all that I will inherit in the life to come is in Jesus and because of Him. Certainly if I had my just reward I would already be screaming in hell; but through God's mercy and by His grace I now have eternal life, I am now a son of God — and I have been remembered in God's will. I am joint-heir with the Lord Jesus Christ, my inheritance is in Him, and that inheritance is incorruptible, undefiled, and will never fade away. It is reserved and protected in heaven where moths and rust cannot corrupt and thieves. cannot break through and steal. It is in a place of absolute security, an eternal inheritance reserved in heaven for all who have trusted in the finished work of Jesus.

But when I get to heaven, I shall not be too concerned about seeing my mansion, I shall not be too concerned about seeing the street of pure gold or my loved ones and friends who await me there. When I step through the pearly gates the cry of my heart will be, "I WANT TO SEE JESUS!" My inheritance is in Him, because of Him, and I want to kiss the scars in His hands, then fall at His feet, look up into His face and say, "Thank you, Lord, for saving my soul!" I am what I am because of Jesus!

Four Things That Can Never Happen to a Believer

FOUR THINGS THAT CAN NEVER HAPPEN
TO A BELIEVER

1. *Believers Shall Never Thirst:*

". . . Whosoever drinketh of the water that I shall give him shall never thirst . . . " (John 4:14). These words were spoken to the woman of Samaria. The story is well known by those of us who read our Bibles and attend church. Jesus was traveling into Galilee, "and He must needs go through Samaria." He came to a city of Samaria called Sychar, near a piece of land that Jacob had given to his son, Joseph. Jacob's well was there. Jesus was weary from His journey, and He sat on the well to rest.

It was about the noon hour, and the disciples had gone into the city to buy bread. While the disciples were gone and Jesus sat alone by the well, a woman came to draw water. It is very unusual for a woman to travel alone in that land. Usually five or six women come to the well together, in either early morning or late afternoon. The actions of this woman were unusual: She traveled alone, and she came to draw water at the sixth hour-twelve o'clock noon.

When the woman approached, Jesus opened the conversation. He said to her, "Give me a drink." The woman was astonished, and she asked, "How is it that thou, being a Jew, askest drink of me, which am a woman of Samaria? for the Jews have no dealings with the Samaritans." She was certainly telling the truth. Bible antiquity tells us that the Jews hated the Samaritans so bitterly that they prayed for God to deliver them from the very sight of a Samaritan. But this Jew was asking a Samaritan woman for a drink of water.

In answer to her question, Jesus said, "If thou knewest the gift of God, and who it is that saith to thee, Give me to drink; thou wouldest have asked of him, and he would have given thee living water." Such a statement stirred the woman's curiosity; she must have asked many questions in her own mind. This Jew had just said to her, *"If you knew the gift of God,"* and that certainly indicated ignorance on her part. He then said, *"If you knew who I am,* you would ask of me, and I would give you living water." In a kind, gentle way, this Jew had declared her to be ignorant—both concerning the things of God and concerning His identity. But if His words offended her she gave no sign of it. She simply asked, "Sir, thou hast nothing to draw with and the well is deep: from whence then hast thou that living water? Art thou greater than our father Jacob, which gave us the well?"

Jesus could have said, "Yes, *I AM much greater* than Jacob. I was *before* Jacob." He could have started a red-hot religious argument—but He did not. Had He done so, He might have lost His opportunity to save this poor, fallen woman. Jesus did not come into the world to destroy men's lives; *He came to seek and to save*—and he never missed an opportunity to fulfill His mission. He answered the woman in these words: "Whosoever drinketh of this water shall thirst again: *But whosoever drinketh of the water that I shall give him shall never thirst;* but the water that I shall give him shall be in him a well of water springing up into everlasting life."

Surely this statement further stirred the woman's curiosity—and yet, she could not escape the earnestness and sincerity of this Jew. She could not laugh in His face nor could she ignore Him. There was something very extraordinary about Him; He was like no other person she had ever met. So she said to Him, "Sir, *give*

166

me this water, that I thirst not, neither come hither
to draw."

Step by step, Jesus had led this woman of Samaria
to the very door of salvation. He had laid the foundation
for her to make the final request which would cause her
to become no longer a hated Samaritan, but a daughter
of the living God. Jesus knew her heart, He knew her
sin. He knew that she was living with a man to whom
she was not married, and He knew that she had five
living husbands. When she said, "Give me this water,"
He replied, "Go call thy husband, and come hither."

She promptly confessed, *"I HAVE no husband."* Then
Jesus said, "Thou hast well said . . . For thou hast had five
husbands; and he whom thou now hast is not thy husband:
in that saidst thou truly." When Jesus said that, the
woman declared, *"Sir, I perceive that thou art a prophet."*

At this point, the devil tried to sidetrack the conversation. The woman said, "Our fathers worshipped in this
mountain; and ye say, that in Jerusalem is the place
where men ought to worship." Jesus stopped that line
of thought immediately by telling her that *she was not
ready* to worship *anywhere.* She needed a Saviour. He
said, "Ye worship ye know not what: We know what we
worship: for salvation is of the Jews. But the hour
cometh, and now is, when the true worshippers shall
worship the Father in spirit and in truth; for the Father
seeketh such to worship Him. God is a Spirit: and they
that worship Him must worship Him in spirit and in
truth."

Then the woman gave a testimony which revealed
previous religious training. She said, "I know that
Messiah cometh, which is called Christ: when He is come,
He will tell us all things." How this dear woman learned
about Messiah we will not know until we get to heaven.

The Holy Spirit did not see fit to record who taught her that Messiah would come. Personally, I love to think that she had a God-fearing mother who taught her from the Holy Scriptures; but regardless of how she learned it, she knew that Messiah was coming, and she confessed this knowledge.

Jesus could have begun in Genesis and preached through Malachi—but He did not. This dear woman was thirsty, and He had promised to give her living water. So when she confessed, "I know that Messiah is coming," Jesus knew that she was ready to drink from the fountain of living water; and He said, *"I that speak unto thee am He!"* These seven words contained an artesian well; The woman had said, "I know Messiah cometh." Jesus replied, "I that speak unto thee am He," she believed His words— and He saved her that very moment. "The woman then left her waterpot, and went her way into the city, and saith to the men, Come, see a man, which told me all things that ever I did. IS NOT THIS THE CHRIST?" (John 4.28; 29).

She asked for living water, and Jesus GAVE her living water—He gave her water that was not from Jacob's well: *"Whosoever drinketh of the water that I shall give him shall never thirst."* We have assurance that those who come to Christ and drink of the living water shall never thirst: they shall drink, and drink, and drink, forever and ever; because when Jesus saves us, He puts within our bosom an artesian well that springs up and keeps on springing up—and we keep on drinking.

"But whosoever drinketh of the water that I shall give him shall never thirst; but the water that I shall give him shall be in him a well of water springing up into everlasting life" (John 4:14).

Here we have an emphatic, positive statement: *"Whosoever"* takes in everyone and excludes no one, regardless of nationality, creed, or color. "Whosoever *drinketh"* means to exercise faith in the shed blood, believe on the Lord Jesus Christ, and trust Him as personal Saviour. In other words, we not only believe that there IS living water but we DRINK of that water; and *whosoever drinks of the water Jesus gives shall never thirst again.* This is heavenly water, divine, living water; it is not religion, dogma, doctrine, or tradition. *Now what IS the water Jesus Gives?*

Jesus gave the woman water—*He gave her His WORD:* "I that speak unto thee am He!"

"Except a man be born of the water and of the Spirit, he cannot enter into the kingdom of God" (John 3:5). (This water is not the baptistry or the river Jordan: it is the *Word of God.)*

"Now ye are clean through the *Word* which I have spoken unto you" (John 15:3).

"That He might sanctify and cleanse it with the washing of water by the *Word"* (Eph. 5:26).

"Being born again, not of corruptible seed, but of incorruptible, by the *Word of God,* which liveth and abideth for ever" (I Pet. 1:23).

From these Scriptures we see that the water is definitely the Word, and that is what Jesus gave the woman at the well.

"Verily, verily, I say unto you, He that heareth my Word, and believeth on Him that sent me, hath everlasting life, and shall not come into condemnation, but is passed from death unto life" (John 5:24).

"For by grace are ye saved through faith; and that not of yourselves: it is the gift of God: not of works, lest any man should boast" (Eph. 2:8, 9).

169

"So then faith cometh by hearing, and hearing by the Word of God" (Rom. 10:17).

That settles it!!! The true believer *shall never thirst.*

2. *Believers Shall Never Hunger:*

". . . Jesus said unto them, I am the bread of life: he that cometh to me shall never hunger" (John 6:35). This memorable passage in the salvation Gospel begins with the account of the feeding of five thousand hungry men (not counting women and children) when, from a little boy's lunch of five barley loaves and two small fishes, Jesus fed the hungry multitude and had twelve baskets of fragments left over.

The next day, the people again sought Jesus, and finally found Him on the other side of the sea. In answer to their questions, He said:

"Verily, verily, I say unto you, Ye seek me, not because ye saw the miracles, but because ye did eat the loaves, and were filled. Labour not for the meat which perisheth, but for that meat which endureth unto everlasting life, which the Son of man shall give unto you: for Him hath God the father sealed. Then said they unto Him, What shall we do, that we might work the works of God? Jesus answered and said unto them, This is the work of God, *that ye believe on Him whom He hath sent.* They said therefore unto Him, What sign shewest thou then, that we may see, and believe thee? What dost thou work? Our fathers did eat manna in the desert; as it is written, He gave them bread from heaven to eat."

This opened the door for Jesus to tell them who He really was: "Then Jesus said unto them, Verily, verily, I say unto you, Moses gave you not that bread from haeven; but my Father giveth you the true bread from heaven" (John 6:22-32 in part).

These people said that *Moses* had given them bread from heaven; but Jesus declared that Moses did NOT give them that bread. Said He, *"My Father* giveth you *the true bread* from heaven. For *the bread of God is He which cometh down from heaven,* and giveth life unto the world." Jesus was referring to Himself, in an attempt to get these poor, lost people to see that *He was their Messiah,* their Saviour. *He was "that Bread from heaven."*

They said to Him, "Lord, evermore give us this bread." And Jesus answered, *"I AM THE BREAD OF LIFE: he that cometh to me shall never hunger; and he that believeth on me shall never thirst."* Jesus exploded a Gospel bombshell here, because these people did not believe that He was the Son of God. He had already, through many miracles, proved to them that He was not an ordinary man. He said, ". . . Ye also have seen me, and believe not. All that the Father giveth me shall come to me; and him that cometh to me I will in no wise cast out. For I came down from heaven, not to do mine own will, but the will of Him that sent me. And this is the Father's will which hath sent me, that of all which He hath given me I should lose nothing, but should raise it up again at the last day. And this is the will of Him that sent me, that every one which seeth the Son, and believeth on Him, may have everlasting life: and I will raise Him up at the last day" (John 6: 35-40).

When Jesus made that clear, bold, divine declaration, the Jews began to murmur and to stir up strife, animosity, and hatred against Him: "The Jews then murmured at Him, because He said, I am the bread which came down from heaven. And they said, Is not this Jesus, the son of Joseph, whose father and mother we know? How is it then that He saith, I came down from heaven? Jesus therefore answered and said unto them, Murmur not among yourselves. No man can come to me, except the Father which hath sent me draw him: and I will raise him up at the last day . . . Verily, verily, I say unto you, He that believeth on me hath everlasting life. I AM THAT BREAD OF LIFE. Your fathers did eat manna in the wilderness, and are dead. THIS IS THE BREAD WHICH COMETH DOWN FROM HEAVEN, that a man may eat thereof, and not die. I AM THE LIVING BREAD which came down from heaven: if any man eat of this bread, HE SHALL LIVE FOR EVER: and the bread that I will give is my flesh, which I will give for the life of the world.

"The Jews therefore strove among themselves, saying, *How can this man give us His flesh to eat?*" The natural man does not receive the things of God, for they are spiritually discerned and he cannot know them. These men were looking only in the natural realm. They were looking for a great earthly ruler, someone who would be their leader to overthrow the Romans and take back their land. They were looking for a glamorous, powerful, king to rule and destroy the Romans.

But Jesus answered them by saying, "Verily, verily, I say unto you, Except ye eat the flesh of the Son of man, and drink His blood, ye have no life in you. Whoso eateth my flesh, and drinketh my blood, hath eternal life; and I will raise him up at the last day. For my flesh is meat indeed, and my blood is drink indeed. He that eateth my flesh, and drinketh my blood, dwelleth in me, and I in him. As the living Father hath sent me, and I live by the Father: so he that eateth me, even he shall live by me. THIS IS THAT BREAD WHICH CAME DOWN FROM HEAVEN: not as your fathers did eat manna, and are dead: he that eateth of this bread shall live for ever. These things said He in the synagogue, as He taught in Capernaum" (John 6:41-59).

After Jesus spoke these tremendous words, many of his followers said, "This is a hard saying; who can hear it? . . . and from that time many of his disciples went back, and walked no more with Him."

Jesus knew what they were saying—He knew their very thoughts. He turned to the twelve and asked, "WILL YE ALSO GO AWAY?"

"Then Simon Peter answered Him, *Lord, to whom shall we go?* Thou hast the words of eternal life! "And we believe and are sure that thou art that Christ, the Son of the living God!" (John 6:60-69 in part).

For a more detailed account of these happenings, read the entire sixth chapter of John; we have quoted only portions of it. This has always been one of my favorite chapters in the Word of God. Jesus IS the Bread of Life, HE DID come down from the heavenly Father, and several times in this wonderful chapter He reiterates the fact that He came from God, and that He came to satisfy the soul-hunger of poor, lost mankind. But the statement that really caused the Jews to turn against Him was when He told them, "Except ye eat the flesh of the Son of man, and drink His blood, ye have no life in you." Had they been willing to receive Jesus they could have understood that statement.

"In the beginning was the Word, and the Word was with God, and the Word was God . . . and the Word was made flesh, and dwelt among us, (and we beheld His glory, the glory as of the only begotten of the Father,) full of grace and truth" (John 1:1 and 14).

In the beginning, *The Word WAS*, and the Word was *GOD*, and *the Word became flesh*. JESUS was the Word in flesh, and when He said, "Except ye eat my flesh and drink my blood," He simply meant, "Except you assimilate my Word, except you take my Word into your very soul, *you have no life.*"

Just as the Word is the living water, it is also the living bread; and when we *hear* the word, *believe* the word, and *receive* the Word, *the engrafted Word brings life.* We are begotten through the Word because the Word brings faith, and *faith exercised* brings salvation. The Word washes us clean, the Word is the *incorruptible seed* that "borns" us into the family of God. Paul said, "I am not ashamed of the Gospel (the Word) of Christ: for it is the power of God unto salvation to every one that believeth; to the Jew first, and also to the Greek" (Rom. 1:16).

These Jews were religious but lost. They thought they knew SO much—yet they were totally ignorant—many of them willingly so—concerning their Messiah. They had seen His miracles, had heard His wonderful words of life, but they refused to believe on Him. In John 5:40 He said to this same class of people, *"And ye will not come to me, that ye might have life."*

Dear reader, have you eaten of the bread of life? If not, *you HAVE no life,* you are spiritually dead. This moment, if you will believe on the Lord Jesus Christ, believe and receive His Word and you shall have everlasting life. Not only will you have everlasting life, but all that your poor soul will ever need or crave, you will find in Jesus. He is the living Bread, the bread which makes alive and satisfies the soul. He is the only Bread that CAN satisfy the hungry soul. In Him—and in Him alone—we find hunger satisfied continually—day by day, week by week, and year after year until we are safe in the Paradise of God. He satisfies in peace, joy, and fullness. He is able to do for us exceeding abundantly above anything we could ever hope, think, or ask. He is the all-sufficient

Saviour, in Him our every need is supplied, and in Him we are complete (Col. 2:9, 10).

3. *Believers Shall Never Be Forsaken*:

"Let your conversation be without covetousness; and be content with such things as ye have: for He hath said, *I will never leave thee, nor forsake thee,* so that we may boldly say, The Lord is my helper, and I will not fear what man shall do unto me" (Heb. 13:5, 6).

What a precious truth! What wonderful assurance! We know that Christ will never leave us, He will never forsake us, He will tenderly watch over us every step of the way. It is possible for our very best friends to leave us, forsake us, and forget us; but it is impossible for Christ to forsake us or leave us, because He promised—and He cannot lie (Heb. 6:18; Titus 1:2). He will never forsake us in life, in death, nor in eternity!

"If God be for us, who can be against us?" You and Jesus make a majority over any crowd —yea, the whole world. To His disciples Jesus said, "In the world ye shall have tribulation: but be of good cheer; I have overcome the world" (John 16:33). I am so thankful for Jesus— thankful that He came into the world, lived here, walked here, was tempted here, and tasted life in every respect as we taste life—yet He never sinned. Of His enemies He asked, "Which one of you convinceth me of sin?" and not one could point a finger of accusation at Jesus Christ. He overcame the world, the flesh, and the devil. And through Him, *we are more than conquerors!* (Rom. 8:37).

On the Mount of Temptation Satan met Jesus personally and hurled at Him everything hell had. He tempted Him through the lust of the flesh, the lust of the eye, and the pride of life. Jesus withstood every temptation, and when the devil departed, angels came and ministered unto

175

Him. (Read the story in Matthew 4:1-11.)

Satan is a defeated foe—and he knows it; but he was not defeated by you nor by me. He was defeated by our wonderful Lord who promised, "I will never leave thee nor forsake thee!"

As long as we remain in the flesh, we will be tested, tried, and tempted; but we have this precious promise: "There hath no temptation taken you but such as is common to man: but God is faithful, who will not suffer you to be tempted above that ye are able; but will with the temptation also make a way to escape, that ye may be able to bear it" (Cor. 10:13).

What a promise! He who said, "I will never leave thee nor forsake thee" also declares in His precious Word that there can no temptation overtake us but what is common temptation to *all* men. The devil has no new tricks. After six thousands years' experience in damning souls, he still uses the same methods, the same avenues of approach, that he used in the Garden of Eden! He tempted Eve through the lust of the eye, the lust of the flesh and the pride of life. (She looked at the forbidden fruit, she desired it for food, she was ambitious to be wise.) Satan still tempts through those same avenues:

"Love not the world, neither the things that are in the world. If any man love the world, the love of the Father is not in him. For all that is in the world, *the lust of the flesh and the lust of the eyes, and the pride of life,* is not of the Father, but is of the world" (I John 2:15, 16).

The Word tells us that no temptation will overtake us but such as is common to all men; but here is the heart of the promise: *"GOD IS FAITHFUL!"* We can rely upon the faithfulness of God. Because He IS GOD, he cannot go back on His Word: *"If we believe not, yet He abideth faithful: He cannot deny Himself"* (II Tim. 2:13).

Greek scholars tell us that this verse reads, "If we believe not, yet He abideth faithful. He cannot take back what HE has said." The God who loved us enough to give Jesus to die for us will surely keep His promise to us. He will never forsake us, and He will never permit us to be tempted above what we are able to bear. The believer who falls into sin has no one to blame but himself. He cannot blame his fellowman—and he certainly cannot blame God!

In I Corinthians 10:12 Paul warns, ". . . . Let him that thinketh he standeth take heed lest he fall." The moment we put confidence in the flesh we are headed for sure defeat. We need to learn with Paul, that in us (in our flesh) dwells no good thing (Rom. 7:18). When we learn this tremendous truth, we will be victorious over the world, the flesh, and the devil. Every believer should remember that when we are born again, it is the *spirit* that is born of God; the flesh is not changed. Before conversion, the believer has only one nature; after conversion he has two natures—the flesh and the spirit, the earthly and the divine, warring against each other.

Man is a fallen creature, and with his fallen nature the only way to overcome the flesh is to submit soul, spirit, and body to God, yielding our members as instruments of righteousness unto holiness. The flesh is the enemy of the believer, and we must *deal* with it as an enemy:

"And God looked upon the earth, and, behold, it was corrupt; for all flesh had corrupted his way upon the earth" (Gen. 6:12).

"But we are all as an unclean thing, and all our righteousnesses are as filthy rags" (Isa. 64:6).

"They are all gone aside, they are altogether become filthy; there is none that doeth good, no, not one" (Psalm 14:3).

"And they that are Christ's have crucified the flesh with the affections and lusts" (Gal. 5:24).

"For the flesh lusteth against the Spirit, and the Spirit against the Flesh: and these are contrary the one to the other: so that ye cannot do the things that ye would" (Gal. 5:17).

"Now the works of the flesh are manifest, which are these: Adultery, fornication, uncleanness, lasciviousness, idolatry, witchcraft, hatred, variance, emulations, wrath, strife, seditions, heresies, envyings, murders, drunkenness, revellings, and such like: of the which I tell you before, as I have also told you in time past, that they which do such things shall not inherit the kingdom of God" (Gal. 5:19-21).

"So then they that are in the flesh cannot please God" (Rom. 8:8).

"For if ye live after the flesh, ye shall die: but if ye through the Spirit do mortify the deeds of the body, ye shall live" (Rom. 8:13).

"That no flesh should glory in His presence. But of Him are ye in Christ Jesus, who of God is made unto us wisdom, and righteousness, and sanctification, and redemption" (I Cor. 1:29, 30).

"Having therefore these promises, dearly beloved, let us cleanse ourselves from all filthiness of the flesh and spirit, perfecting holiness in the fear of God" (II Cor. 7:1).

"For we are the circumcision, which worship God in the spirit, and rejoice in Christ Jesus, and have no confidence in the flesh" (Phil. 3:3).

"For if the blood of bulls and of goats, and the ashes of an heifer sprinkling the unclean, sanctifieth to the purifying of the flesh: How much more shall the blood of Christ, who through the eternal Spirit offered Himself without spot to God, purge your conscience from dead works to serve the living God?" (Heb. 9:13, 14).

If you as a believer have realized these things about the flesh you are a victorious and happy Christian, enjoying your spiritual birthright.

"Now thanks be unto God, which always causeth us to triumph in Christ, and maketh manifest the savour of His knowledge by us in every place" (II Cor. 2:14).

"I can do all things through Christ which strengtheneth me" (Phil. 4:13).

". . . My God shall supply all your need according to His riches in glory by Christ Jesus" (Phil. 4:19).

David, a man after God's own heart, testified, "I have been young, and now am old; yet have I not seen the righteous forsaken, nor his seed begging bread" (Psalm 37:25).

Jesus said to His disciples, "Have faith in God" (Mark 11:22). If we have faith in God we have nothing to fear —in this life, nor in the life to come. He who promised, "I will never leave thee nor forsake thee" will go with us all the way, even to the end; and then . . . "Yea, though I walk through the valley of the shadow of death, I will fear no evil: for thou art with me!" (Psalm 23:4).

Jesus resurrects us from spiritual death when we believe on Him (Eph. 2:1). He leads us safely around the pitfalls and through whatever temptations the devil and hell hurl at us (I Cor. 10: 13). And then when we come down to die, He walks with us—not INTO, but THROUGH—the valley of the shadow of death. He leads us through the valley and out on the other side—*into the Paradise of God!*

Believers need not fear death. We do not *look forward* to death, but we are not afraid to die, because we know Him who said, "I am He that liveth, and was dead! and, behold, I am alive for evermore, Amen; and have the keys of hell and of death" (Rev. 1:18). I know my Lord Jesus has the key to death and hell and I know that He will walk with me through the valley of the shadow of death—so why should I be afraid? The Christ in whom I have put my trust is able to keep me, walk with me, confess me to the heavenly Father, and present me faultless before Him. Therefore, I do not fear the past—for Jesus, in His death, burial, and resurrection "according to the Scriptures" has already taken care of past sins. He has redeemed us by His blood. I do not fear the present— for my Advocate takes care of that (I John 2:1, 2). I do not fear the future—for Jesus has already taken care of my needs for time and eternity:

"In my Father's house are many mansions . . . I go to prepare a place for *you*" (John 14:1-6 in part). Jesus is preparing a home for the bride, the New Testament church; and He is also preparing an incorruptible body for every saint—a body like unto His glorious resurrection body: "Beloved, now are we the sons of God, and it doth not yet appear what we shall be; but we know that, when He shall appear, we shall like Him; for we shall see Him as He is" (John 3:2).

The God who promised, "I will never leave thee nor forsake thee" is very capable of seeing us safely into Paradise, He is able to supply our every need until we arrive there, and He will provide for every need we may have throughout all eternity. Hallelujah! What a Saviour! What a keeper, what a Confessor! I am so glad I know Jesus! Do you know Him? If you do not know Him, He will save you now, this very moment, if you will only trust Him.

4. *Believers Shall Never Perish*:

"And I give unto them eternal life; and they shall never perish, neither shall any man pluck them out of my hand" (John 10:28).

In the opening verses of the tenth chapter of John's Gospel, Jesus gives His discourse on the Good Shepherd:

"Verily, verily, I say unto you, He that entereth not by the door into the sheepfold, but climbeth up some other way, the same is a thief and a robber. But he that entereth in by the door is the shepherd of the sheep. To him the porter openeth; and the sheep hear his voice: and he calleth his own sheep by name, and leadeth them out. And when he putteth forth his own sheep, he goeth before them, and the sheep follow him: for they know his voice. *And a stranger will they not follow*, but will flee from him: *for they know not the voice of strangers*" (John 10: 1-5).

Here, Jesus presents Himself as the Good Shepherd, the Door to the sheepfold. But the tremendous part of His statement, a declaration that every believer should commit to memory, lies in these words: "A STRANGER THEY WILL NOT FOLLOW, BUT WILL FLEE FROM HIM: FOR THEY KNOW NOT THE VOICE OF STRANGERS!" According to this Scripture, sheep do not follow strangers—*they run from them*. Therefore, dearly beloved, we may know those who follow every cult, false doctrine, religion or "ism" that passes through the community are not sheep—and never were! Jesus said, "MY sheep will not follow a stranger. They will run from him because they do not know his voice."

He also said, "I am the door: by me if any man enter in, he shall be saved, and shall go in and out, and find pasture . . . I am the Good Shepherd: the good shepherd giveth his life for the sheep" (John 10:9, 11).

181

He then tells us why the heavenly Father loves Him so much: "I am the Good Shepherd, and know my sheep, and am known of mine. As the Father knoweth me, even so know I the Father: and I lay down my life for the sheep. And other sheep I have, which are not of this fold: them also I must bring, and they shall hear my voice; and there shall be one fold, and one shepherd.

"Therefore doth my Father love me, because I lay down my life, that I might take it again. No man taketh it from me, but I lay it down of myself. I have power to lay it down, and I have power to take it again. This commandment have I received of my Father.

"There was a division therefore again among the Jews for these sayings. And many of them said, He hath a devil, and is mad; why hear ye Him? Others said, These are not the words of him that hath a devil. Can a devil open the eyes of the blind?" (John 10:14-21).

In Jerusalem at the feast of the dedication, the Jews came to Jesus and said, *"If thou be the Christ, tell us plainly."* Jesus replied, "I told you, and ye believed not: the works that I do in my Father's name, they bear witness of me. But ye believe not, because ye are not of my sheep, as I said unto you." In other words, Jesus said to them, "You have seen my miracles, you have heard my words of life, and you will not believe. If I should say to you plainly, 'I am your Messiah, I am the Son of God', you would not believe me."

Then He said:

"My sheep hear my voice,
and I know them,
   and they follow me:
And I give unto them eternal life;
and they shall never perish,
neither shall any man pluck them out of my hand.

My Father, which gave them to me, is greater than all; and no man is able to pluck them out of my Father's hand. I and my Father are one" (John 10:27-30).

I see no need to comment on these clear words of Gospel truth. Read them, re-read them—and then read them again! And as you read, pray for God to open the eyes of your understanding that He may reveal to you the tremendous truth laid down in these verses.

Believers are born of God—John 1:13.

Believers are raised with Christ to walk in newness of life—Rom. 6:4.

Positionally, believers are seated with Jesus in heavenly places—Eph. 2:6.

Believers are sealed until the day of redemption—Eph. 4:30.

Believers are dead, and their lives are hid with Christ in God—Col. 3:3.

The life of a believer is in the Lord Jesus Christ—Col. 3:4.

Believers are new creations—II Cor. 5:17.

Believers are free from all condemnation—Rom. 8:1.

Believers can cry out to all the earth, to all the underworld, and to all heaven:

"WHO SHALL SEPARATE US FROM THE LOVE OF CHRIST? Shall
      tribulation,
      or distress,
      or persecution,
      or famine,
      or nakedness.
      or peril,
      or sword?

As it is written, For thy sake we are killed all the day long; we are accounted as sheep for the slaughter. Nay, in all these things we are more than conquerors through Him that loved us. For I am persuaded, that neither *death*, nor *life*, nor *angels*, nor *principalities*, nor *powers*, nor *things present*, nor *things to come*, nor *height*, nor *depth*, NOR *ANY OTHER CREATURE*, shall be able to separate us from the love of God, which is in Christ Jesus our Lord!" (Rom. 8:35-39).

That settles it! That takes in everything, it excludes nothing. Dearly beloved, if you are not saved, these precious verses from God's Word should convict you of your need for salvation, and convince you that through faith in Jesus Christ you can have *eternal life*. If these verses do not convince you, then I am sure that nothing I could say would change your mind.

If you ARE saved, then comfort your heart with these blessed truths:

Believers are God's children now: "NOW are we the sons of God."

Believers are partakers of divine nature NOW: "Whereby are given unto us exceeding great and precious promises: that by these ye might be partakers of the divine nature, having escaped the corruption that is in the world through lust" (II Pet. 1:4).

Believers shall never perish: we are kept by the power of God: "Blessed be the God and Father of our Lord Jesus Christ, which according to His abundant mercy hath begotten us again unto a lively hope by the resurrection of Jesus Christ from the dead, to an inheritance incorruptible, and undefiled, and that fadeth not away, reserved in heaven for you, WHO ARE KEPT BY THE POWER OF GOD through faith unto salvation ready to be revealed in the last time" (I Pet. 1:3-5).

As a closing testimony in this message, let us listen to the Apostle Paul, the man whom God called and ordained a minister to the Gentiles: "For the which cause I also suffer these things: nevertheless I am not ashamed: FOR I KNOW WHOM I HAVE BELIEVED, and am persuaded that HE IS ABLE TO KEEP that which I have committed unto Him against that day!" (II Tim. 1:12).

My precious reader, if you live in constant fear lest you not live good enough, afraid that you will not hold out or that you will not make it to heaven, surely the devil has slipped you a counterfeit. If you *are* trusting in Jesus, remember His promise, *"I will never leave thee nor forsake thee"*— and He will not break His promise, He cannot lie. He promises no temptation can come to you but that God will with the temptation make a way of escape, that you may be able to bear it. He promises to supply your every need—physical, spiritual, and eternal.

Christian, do not fear: "There is no fear in love; but perfect love casteth out fear: because fear hath torment. He that feareth is not made perfect in love" (I John 4:18). It is a sin to doubt God and fear that He will not keep you or that He will not supply the needed grace to live a victorious Christian life. Believers have the Word of God to stand upon—is that not sufficient? He promised, *"They* (the born again ones) *shall never perish!"* Believe that promise fully—and you will live in the suburbs of Paradise until you arrive there to spend eternity!

Ten Present Possessions of the Believer

TEN PRESENT POSSESSIONS
OF THE BELIEVER

1. *Believers Have God's Seal Upon the Heart*:

"And grieve not the holy Spirit of God, whereby ye are sealed unto the day of redemption" (Eph. 4:30).

Every *country* and state has a royal seal, every *corporation* has a seal. God has sealed every child of His, and He knows His own because of the seal He places upon them when they are born again. This verse of Scripture clearly points out that believers bear the identification of the seal, and we are clearly told for *how long* we are sealed:

The seal of God is the *Spirit* of God. When an unbeliever is convicted of sin and comes to the Lord Jesus Christ, believing that HE IS Christ—crucified, buried, and risen "according to the Scriptures," that unbeliever is born again, thus becoming a Christian; and the split second he is born again, the Holy Spirit takes up His abode in the heart. ". . . If any man have not the Spirit of Christ, he is none of His " (Rom. 8:8b). "For as many as are led by the Spirit of God, they are the sons of God . . . The Spirit itself beareth witness with our spirit, that we are the children of God" (Rom. 8:14 and 16).

There is no such thing as salvation apart from the Holy Spirit. He not only draws us, convicts us, "borns" us into the family of God, indwells us, leads us and assures us, but He also SEALS us.

Every true believer possesses the seal of God now—*but for how long?* The Scripture answers, "UNTO THE DAY OF REDEMPTION!" I am so glad God does not save the sinner and then *leave it up to the sinner* to make it to heaven! I am so glad God does not save us, and then turn us loose among the spiritual wolves of the world to take care of *ourselves*. God saves us, indwells us, and puts His seal upon us—and you may rest assured that Satan knows when a person is God's property.

The reason the devil has no trouble tripping many church members and causing them to stumble and fall is that he comes to the heart and finds no seal on it. Jesus gives the account of such a man in Matthew 12: 43-45:

"When the unclean spirit is gone out of a man, he walketh through dry places, seeking rest, and findeth none. Then he saith, I will return into my house from whence I came out; and when he is come, he findeth it empty, swept, and garnished. Then goeth he, and taketh with himself seven other spirits more wicked than himself, and they enter in and dwell there: and the last state of that man is worse than the first."

In these verses we have an illustration of the worthlessness of self-reformation. This man decided that he would reform and live a better life. So the unclean spirit left him, walked "through dry places, seeking rest, and findeth none." Then the unclean spirit said, "I will return into MY house from whence I came out." And when he returned to HIS house he found it "EMPTY, swept and garnished." There was no seal on the door, and he had no difficulty in re-entering the house. And when he entered the second time *into his own house,* he took with him seven other spirits more wicked than himself! They entered the house and dwelt there, and the last state of that man was worse than the first!

Please note that the unclean spirit said, "My house." When a person is truly *born again* he is no longer the property of the devil. He is not inhabited by unclean spirits. He is God's purchased possession, God's child, and he bears the seal of the Holy Spirit.

It makes no difference how clean one may make himself by reforming, he is still wicked in the sight of God. Christ is made unto us righteousness, and the only person who is made righteous is the person who is in Christ Jesus: "But we are all as an unclean thing, and all our righteousnesses are as filthy rags; and we all do fade as a leaf; and our iniquities, like the wind, have taken us away" (Isa. 64:6). The only righteousness God honors is Jesus Christ.

A seal is a mark of ownership and recognition. Every born again, blood-washed believer is sealed by the Holy Spirit. *WHEN does God seal the believer?* Ephesians 1:13 answers:

"In whom ye also trusted, after that ye heard the word of truth, the Gospel of your salvation: in whom also *after that ye believed, ye were SEALED with the Holy Spirit of promise."*

The Ephesian Christians had trusted in the Lord Jesus Christ, they had believed the message of grace delivered by the Apostle Paul. They had heard the Word of truth (faith comes by hearing, and hearing by the Word). And when they believed in Christ, they were sealed with the Holy Spirit. The sealing, which is the mark of ownership, takes place immediately upon exercising faith in Jesus unto salvation. When the Ephesians heard the Gospel of truth, and believed that Gospel, they were saved *and sealed with the Holy Spirit of promise.* The sealing takes place in the heart of the believer today, just as it did in the days of the Apostle Paul. God has not changed His method or His program as having to do with our salvation.

God's Part in the Sealing

What part does God the Father play in our salvation insofar as the sealing of the Holy Spirit is concerned? II Timothy 2:19 answers:

"Nevertheless, THE FOUNDATION OF GOD standeth sure, having this seal, The Lord knoweth them that are His."

"For other foundation can no man lay than that is laid, which is Jesus Christ" (I Cor. 3:11).

The foundation of Christianity is Christ. "Christ in you, the hope of glory" (Col. 1:27). God is the author, the originator, and the giver of the grace that brought salvation down to man and made it possible for us to be placed upon the foundation of God—the Lord Jesus Christ. And having this seal, *the Lord knoweth them that are His.*

In Matthew 7:24-27 Jesus speaks of two foundations: "Therefore whosoever heareth these sayings of mine, and doeth them, I will liken him unto a wise man, which built his house upon a rock: And the rain descended, and the floods came, and the winds blew, and beat upon that house; and it fell not: for it was founded upon a rock. And every one that heareth these sayings of mine, and doeth them not, shall be likened unto a foolish man, which built his house upon the sand: And the rain descended, and the floods came, and the winds blew, and beat upon that house; and it fell: and great was the fall of it."

When Jesus finished this sermon, the Pharisees declared that He taught as one having authority, and they were astonished at His doctrine. You will note that Jesus mentioned no part of the house except the foundation. He did not mention the floor, the sub-floor, the walls, the ceiling, the roof. He simply mentioned the foundation. We know that if the foundation of a building is faulty, then regardless of how strong the construction may be throughout the rest of the house, it will not stand.

The same is true of religion. There are many beautiful religions, and there are many good points in many religions; but Christianity is the only one with a sure foundation. Christianity is the only religion which is founded upon Jesus Christ.

Dear reader, if you are building upon the Lord Jesus,

that means that you have trusted Him, you are IN CHRIST, He is in you—and having this seal upon your heart, the Lord knows you and you know Him. I believe that if you are saved, you know it. I doubt that there is such a thing as salvation apart from assurance. To Timothy Paul said, *". . . I know WHOM I have believed, and am persuaded* that He is able to keep that which I have committed unto Him against that day"* (II Tim. 1:12).

In I John 3:14 the Word tells us, *"We KNOW that we have passed from death unto life because we love the brethren. He that loveth not his brother abideth in death."*

We who are saved can say with the man to whom Jesus gave sight, ". . . One thing I KNOW, that, whereas I was blind, now I see!" (John 9:25).

"Nevertheless, THE FOUNDATION OF GOD STAND-ETH SURE, having this seal . . ." Are you born of the Spirit—or did the devil slip you a counterfeit? Were you "born"—or did you simply "join"? Are you truly a believer —or are you just a church member? Do you have the assurance of the Spirit IN your heart? If you have the assurance of the Spirit IN your heart, then you have the SEAL of the Spirit ON your heart. If you do not have the assurance and the seal, then you are still the property of Satan. Bow your head, receive Jesus, He will save you and SEAL you —and He will give you blessed assurance.

2. *Believers Have Access To God by Jesus Christ:*

Since we are God's children, indwelt and sealed by the Holy Ghost, we bear God's mark of ownership and recognition and we have the very presence of God Himself.

In the Old Testament era, God appointed and anointed priests to enter into the holy of holies and plead for the people. The priest brought blood—first for himself, and then for the people. But it is different now, because *our* High Priest offered *Himself* — once, forever, never to be repeated. And it is through Him that "we have access by faith into this grace wherein we stand, and rejoice in hope of the glory of God" (Rom. 5:2). Believers do not need an earthly priest to plead for them before God. Since we are sons of God, possessing the Holy Spirit and the seal of God, we ourselves enter boldly into the holy of holies:

"Having therefore, brethren, boldness to enter into the holiest by the blood of Jesus, by a new and living way, which He hath consecrated for us, through the veil, that is to say, His flesh; having an high priest over the house of God; Let us draw near with a true heart in full assurance of faith, having our hearts sprinkled from an evil conscience, and our bodies washed with pure water" (Heb. 10:19-22).

We are invited to come to God through Jesus Christ, whose death on the cross opened up for us *a new and living way.*

Jesus walked and talked with His disciples for three and one-half years. Then one day, He made an announcement that broke their hearts. He told them of His approaching betrayal and His death. Knowing how this disturbed them, He said to them, "Let not your heart be troubled: ye believe in God, believe also in me. In my Father's house are many mansions: if it were not so, I would have told you. I go to prepare a place for you. And if I go and prepare a place for you, I will come again, and receive you unto myself; that where I am, there ye may be also. And whither I go ye know, and the way ye know. Thomas saith unto Him, Lord, we know not whither thou goest; and how can we know the way? Jesus saith unto him, *I am the way, the truth, and the life: no man cometh unto the Father, but by me"* (John 14:1-6).

No man can have access to God except by Jesus Christ. He is the Way—and without the way there is no going. He is the Truth—and without the truth there is no knowing.

Without Jesus there is no hope. Only by Him do we have access to God and to the Father's house.

3. *Believers Have a Great High Priest*:

In Hebrews chapter ten we learn that the law was a shadow of things to come, and the sacrifices offered year by year under the law could not "make the comers thereunto perfect." Those sacrifices only brought remembrance of sin. It was not possible that the blood of bulls and goats should *take away* sins, and God had no pleasure in burnt offerings and sacrifices. Therefore, Jesus came *to take away the first* that He might *establish the second*:

"Then said He, Lo, I come to do thy will, O God. He taketh away the first, that He may establish the second. By the which will we are sanctified through the offering of the body of Jesus Christ once for all. And every priest standeth daily ministering and offering oftentimes the same sacrifices, which can never take away sins: But this man (Jesus), after He had offered one sacrifice for sins for ever, sat down on the right hand of God; From henceforth expecting till His enemies be made His footstool. For by one offering He hath perfected for ever them that are sanctified. Whereof the Holy Ghost also is a witness to us: for after that He had said before, This is the covenant that I will make with them after those days, saith the Lord, I will put my laws into their hearts, and in their minds will I write them; and their sins and iniquities will I remember no more. Now where remission of these is, there is no more offering for sin" (Heb. 10:9-18).

Notice the words in verse 12: "BUT THIS MAN . . ." This Man has spoken a message that no other could speak. This Man has done for us what no other could have done. This Man is to us what no other man could be (I Tim. 2:5). This Man brought God down to us in order that we might comprehend God. This Man WAS very God—yet man. In

195

His death, this Man did what no other could have ever done, living OR dead. And God "hath appointed a day, in the which He will judge the world in righteousness by that Man whom He hath ordained; whereof He hath given assurance unto all men, in that He hath raised Him from the dead" (Acts 17:31).

"Seeing then that we have a great High Priest, that is passed into the heavens, Jesus the Son of God, let us hold fast our profession. For we have not an high priest which cannot be touched with the feeling of our infirmities; but was in all points tempted like as we are, yet without sin. Let us therefore come boldly unto the throne of grace, that we may obtain mercy, and find grace to help in time of need" (Heb. 4:14-16).

"For there is one God, and one Mediator between God and men, the man Christ Jesus, who gave Himself a ransom for all, to be testified in due time" (I Tim. 2:5, 6).

Christ is not only our Redeemer, our Saviour, our Sanctifier, our righteousness, our holiness, our wisdom. He is also our High Priest—and we need none other. I praise God that every believer is invited to enter boldly into the holy of holies "by a new and living way," through our living High Priest, the Man Christ Jesus:

"But ye are a chosen generation, *a royal priesthood,* an holy nation, a peculiar people; that ye should shew forth the praises of Him who hath called you out of darkness into His marvellous light" (I Pet. 2:9).

According to the Word of God, every born again child of God is a priest and we do not need any man to intercede to God in our behalf. We approach God boldly, we enter boldly into the holy of holies through our great High Priest.

"But this Man, because He continueth ever, hath an unchangeable priesthood. Wherefore He is able also to save them to the uttermost that come unto God by Him, seeing

He ever liveth to make intercession for them" (Heb. 7:24, 25).

"For Christ is not entered into the holy places made with hands, which are the figures of the true; but into heaven itself, now to appear in the presence of God for us" (Heb. 9:24).

He is able to save from the "guttermost" to the *uttermost*. Christ is able to save the most ungodly, despicable sinner who ever lived. When a person is so mean, so filthy, so ungodly, debased, and sordid that even the jailer does not want him in his jail, bring that man to Jesus! He is looking for him, He will *save* him, and wash him as white as the driven snow. He is able to save to the uttermost ALL who will come to God by Him. He lives to make intercession for us. He is our Confessor, and in Matthew 10:32 and 33 He tells us, "Whosoever therefore shall confess me before men, him will I confess also before my Father which is in heaven. But whosoever shall deny me before men, him will I also deny before my Father which is in heaven."

4. *Believers Have An Advocate*:

"My little children, these things write I unto you, that ye sin not. And if any man sin, we have an Advocate with the Father, Jesus Christ the righteous: And He is the propitation for our sins: and not for our's only, but also for the sins of the whole world" (I John 2:1 and 2).

God does not give any person a permit or license to practice sin. God hates sin, and *He does not want His children to sin;* but as long as we remain in this tabernacle of flesh we are prone to fall short of God's glory—whether by sin of omission or sin of commission.

Therefore, when the child of God sins (and "whatsoever is not of faith is sin") he knows that he has an Advocate with the Father who will intercede on behalf of the erring one. Through our Advocate we have atonement and we have

197

forgiveness—but ONLY through HIM. It is a comforting truth to know that Jesus not only saves us—but He also confesses us to the Father, and as our heavenly lawyer He pleads our case. He knows the Father better than we can ever know Him this side of heaven. He has pleased the Father, we have *not*. He also knows our needs, He knows our weaknesses. It is the Lord Jesus Christ who pleads our cause and confesses us to the Father. No person on earth can do that!

Since grace abounds, do we practice sin? God forbid! We should not sin just because we have an Advocate in heaven. We should have faith, hope, and trust in Him, we should present our bodies a living sacrifice and our members as instruments of righteousness unto God. *Whatsoever* we do, in word or deed, we should do all to the glory of God, resting in the precious truth that if we do sin and fall short of His glory, we have an Advocate with the Father, *Jesus Christ, the righteous.*

5. *Believers Have an Unction:*

"But ye have an unction from the Holy One, and ye know all things" (I John 2:20).

The unction possessed by the believer is the anointing of the Holy Spirit. He comes into our hearts at the new birth. We are born of the Spirit, indwelt by the Spirit; He is our unction, our anointing—and HE teaches us:

"But the anointing which ye have received of Him abideth in you, and ye need not that any man teach you: but as the same anointing teacheth you of all things, and is truth, and is no lie, and even as it hath taught you, ye shall abide in Him" (I John 2:27).

Believers are taught by the Spirit. All we need to know about God, heaven, Jesus, eternal life or the Holy Spirit is found in God's Word—verbally inspired, dictated by the Holy Ghost to holy men of old who penned down what the

Spirit dictated to them; and since He is the One who GAVE the Word, He is the best teacher OF that Word. There is no better teacher of any book than its author, and the Holy Ghost is the author of the Bible.

"We have also a more sure word of prophecy; whereunto ye do well that ye take heed, as unto a light that shineth in a dark place, until the day dawn, and the day star arise in your hearts: Knowing this first, that no prophecy of the Scripture is of any private interpretation. For the prophecy came not in old time by the will of man: but holy men of God spake as they were moved by the Holy Ghost" (II Pet. 1:19-21).

"All Scripture is given by inspiration of God, and is profitable for doctrine, for reproof, for correction, for instruction in righteousness: That the man of God may be perfect, throughly furnished unto all good works" (II Tim. 3:16, 17).

It is altogether possible for the devil to lead *church members* into error and false doctrine; but a born again, blood-washed child of God will not be confounded and confused by error and the teaching of Satan:

"Wherefore also it is contained in the Scripture, Behold, I lay in Sion a chief corner stone, elect, precious: and he that believeth on Him shall not be confounded" (I Pet. 2:6).

"Now He which stablisheth us with you in Christ, and hath anointed us, is God" (II Cor. 1:21). Every believer is anointed of God, every believer has an unction from the Holy One, and those who are born of the Spirit will not be confused and led about with every wind of doctrine.

6. *Believers Have A Good Conscience*:

"Having a good conscience; that, whereas they speak evil of you, as of evildoers, they may be ashamed that falsely accuse your good conversation in Christ" (I Pet. 3:16).

There are three ways by which we know we are children of God:

(1) Through the Word of God (John 5:24).
(2) Through the witness of the Holy Spirit (Rom. 8:9, 14, 16; Eph. 4:30).
(3) Through the witness of our own heart (I John 3:19-21).

I have purposely listed the *heart* last, because no one except a born again person can trust his own heart. When we believe the Word and the Holy Spirit takes up His abode in our heart, then we can *trust* our heart—but not until then. "The heart is deceitful above all things, and desperately wicked: who can know it?" (Jer. 17:9).

Every believer possesses a spiritual conscience—but let me warn you that if you do not know beyond the shadow of a doubt that you are born again, if you are not living a life consecrated unto God, *do not trust your conscience!* Paul spoke of those who have a conscience seared as with a hot iron—dormant, dead, devoid of sensitivity; but the conscience of a true believer is very sensitive where questionable things are concerned.

In his defence before Felix, Paul said, ". . . Herein do I exercise myself, to have always a conscience void of offence toward God, and toward men" (Acts 24:16). We who name the name of Jesus should so live and conduct ourselves that we will have a good conscience toward God and toward our fellowman. Paul was very careful to point out to believers in the various churches that they must consider those who were outside the Church. Unbelievers watch every move we make, and we must be careful how we live and how we conduct ourselves lest we drive them away from God—which is exactly what the devil would have us do!

Paul could testify, "Men and brethren, I have lived in all good conscience before God until this day" (Acts 23:1). The words of I Timothy 3:9 are included in the qualifications of deacons and elders, but *all believers* should observe them: *"Holding the mystery of the faith in a pure conscience."*

How I thank God that He has put within us that still, small voice of conscience that warns us and is sensitive toward sinful things and questionable habits. If we will but listen to our conscience, dedicated to the Spirit of God, we will have nothing to fear. "For whatsoever is not of faith is sin" (Rom. 14:23 b). What about YOUR conscience, dear reader?

7. *Believers have the Light—The Lord Jesus Christ*:

"That which was from the beginning, which we have heard, which we have seen with our eyes, which we have looked upon, and our hands have handled, of the Word of life; (For the life was manifested, and we have seen it, and bear witness, and shew unto you that eternal life, which was with the Father, and was manifested unto us;) That which we have seen and heard declare we unto you, that ye also may have fellowship with us: and truly our fellowship is with the Father, and with His Son Jesus Christ. And these things write we unto you, that your joy may be full. This then is the message which we have heard of Him, and declare unto you, that God is light, and in Him is no darkness at all. If we say that we have fellowship with Him, and walk in darkness, we lie, and do not the truth: But if we walk in the light, as He is in the light, we have fellowship one with another, and the blood of Jesus Christ His Son cleanseth us from all sin" (I John 1:1-7).

In these verses John says, *"This then is the message:*

(1) God is light.

(2) In Him is no darkness at all.

(3) If we say we have fellowship with Him and walk in darkness, we lie.

(4) If we walk in the light as HE is in the light, we have

201

fellowship one with another. And,

(5) The blood of Jesus Christ His Son cleanseth us from all sin.

Every believer has the Light to guide Him. The psalmist said, "Thy Word is a lamp unto my feet, and a light unto my path" (Psalm 119:105). "The entrance of thy words giveth light" (Psalm 119:130).

"There was a man sent from God, whose name was John. The same came for a witness, to bear witness of the Light, that all men through Him might believe. He was not that Light, but was sent to bear witness of that Light. That was the true Light, which lighteth every man that cometh into the world. He was in the world, and the world was made by Him, and the world knew Him not. He came unto His own, and His own received Him not. But as many as received Him, to them gave He power to become the sons of God, even to them that believe on His name: which were born, not of blood, nor of the will of the flesh, nor of the will of man, but of God" (John 1:6-13).

Christ is our Light. We walk not in darkness; we are led by the Holy Spirit. Light reveals danger, and in Christ we see the snares of the adversary. Insurance companies tell us that light is the cheapest night-protection for our property. Christ is the protection of the believer. He is our salvation, the Light of our life. How this sin-darkened, sin-benighted world needs the light of the Lord Jesus today!

"If ye then be risen with Christ, seek those things which are above, where Christ sitteth on the right hand of God. Set your affection on things above, not on things on the earth. For ye are dead, and your life is hid with Christ in God. When Christ, who is our life, shall appear, then shall ye also appear with Him in glory" (Col. 3:1-4).

8.   *Believers Have Unshakable Confidence In Christ*:

In I John 5:1 we read, "Whosoever believeth that Jesus

is the Christ is born of God: and every one that loveth Him that begat loveth Him also that is begotten of Him." Further on in this chapter, John talks to God's "little children" as the Holy Ghost gives him utterance. He assures us that whosoever is born of God overcomes the world through faith. Who IS he who overcomes the world? *"He that believeth that Jesus is the Son of God."*

He then tells us, "For there are three that bear record in heaven, the Father, the Word, and the Holy Ghost: and these three are one. And there are three that bear witness in earth, the Spirit, and the water, and the blood: and these three agree in one. If we receive the witness of men, the witness of God is greater: for this is the witness of God which He hath testified of His Son. He that believeth on the Son of God hath the witness in himself: he that believeth not God hath made Him a liar; because he believeth not the record that God gave of His Son. And this is the record, that God hath given to us eternal life, and this life is in His Son. He that hath the Son hath life; and he that hath not the Son of God hath not life. These things have I written unto you that believe on the name of the Son of God; that ye may know that ye have eternal life, and that ye may believe on the name of the Son of God. *And this is the confidence that we have in Him, that, if we ask anything according to His will, He heareth us: And if we know that He hear us, whatsoever we ask, we know that we have the petitions that we desired of Him"* (I John 5:7-15).

We have confidence in Christ. We believe on Him unto salvation, we trust Him day by day for victory over the devil. We look to Him to supply our every need—physical, spiritual, mental, or eternal. We who are trusting in Jesus believe that if we pray according to His will He will grant whatsoever we ask (and if we are truly consecrated, we will not ask anything that would be *against* His will). "And we know that all things work together for good to them that love God, to them who are the called according to His purpose" (Rom. 8:28). We may not fully understand this portion of God's Word, but we BELIEVE it, whether we understand it or not.

Prayer in the will of God is the key that unlocks His storehouse and places heaven at our disposal. James 4:2, 3 tells us that we *have* not because we *ask* not, we ask and *receive not* because we ask amiss that we might consume it upon our lusts. In the Sermon on the Mount, Jesus said, "Ask, and it shall be given you; seek, and ye shall find; knock, and it shall be opened unto you: For every one that asketh receiveth; and he that seeketh findeth; and to him that knocketh it shall be opened" (Matt. 7-7, 8).

John 15:7 gives us the precious promise, "If ye abide in me, and my words abide in you, ye shall ask what ye will, and it shall be done unto you."

How do believers know what to pray for or how to make plans? II Timothy 1:7 tells us, "For God hath not given us the spirit of fear; but of power, and of love, and of a sound mind." Hallelujah! God gives us a new heart and a sound mind. "For who hath known the mind of the Lord, that he may instruct him? But we have the mind of Christ" (I Cor. 2:16).

The believer need only to trust in Jesus and rely upon Him as the Spirit leads. God saves—and whom He saves, He directs. "Being confident of this very thing, that He which hath begun a good work in you will perform it until the day of Jesus Christ" (Phil. 1:6). He who purchased our salvation is very capable of directing us around the pitfalls of the devil. Jesus looked into the Father's face and said, "I have finished the work you sent me to do." On three occasions, the heavenly Father audibly stated that He was well pleased with the Son. As for me, I am more than willing to rest my case in the hands of the Son of God who pleased God in every detail!

But hear these precious words: "Likewise the Spirit also helpeth our infirmities: for we know not what we should pray for as we ought: but the Spirit itself maketh intercession for us with groanings which cannot be uttered. And He that searcheth the hearts knoweth what is the mind of the Spirit, because He maketh intercession for the saints according to the will of God" (Rom. 8:26, 27).

The Holy Spirit abides in the bosom of every believer, and He is co-equal with God the Father and God the Son. You cannot separate the Trinity in relation to our salvation. God the Father loved us, God the Son died for us, God the Holy Spirit draws us to Jesus and "borns" us into God's family. Then the Holy Spirit leads us, directs us—and when we pray, He takes over and makes known to God our desires, our longings, our anxieties, our needs, be they great or small. If we are sons of God, led by the Spirit of God, we have nothing to worry about and nothing to fear—for time or for eternity.

9. *Believers Have a Greater Mission Than Angels:*

God could have sent angels to evangelize the world. I am sure a lot of folk would go out to hear an angel preach. If a cherub, a seraph, or the angel Gabriel should come to our city, there is no doubt that large crowds would attend the services. But the unbeliever would then suggest, "Oh, yes! Angels! Certainly *they* can be good and righteous and pure—*but we are men.* We are flesh." But God is sovereign: He knows all things at all times. Therefore, He did what only a sovereign God *could* do to keep men and women out of hell: *He provided salvation in the MAN, Christ Jesus.* Furthermore, He provided an Intercessor, a Mediator. There is a Man in heaven today. God is there, the angels are there, and the spirits of the righteous are there. But there is also

205

a Man, Christ Jesus—the only Mediator between God and men. When Jesus had by Himself purged our sins, He ascended back to the Father and sat down on the right hand of God to plead our case.

Why did God do all of this for poor, hell-deserving sinners? John 15:16 answers: "Ye have not chosen me, but I have chosen you, and ordained you, *that ye should go and bring forth fruit,* and that your fruit should remain: that whatsoever ye shall ask of the Father in my name, He may give it to you."

Believers are chosen and ordained of God to bring forth fruit. It should humble our hearts and make us exceedingly thankful that God Almighty chose man—even you and me —to bear His name, to tell of His love, to point weary sinners to the Saviour, and, through Him, to the heavenly home. If God chose me to bear fruit, then *woe unto me if I FAIL to bear fruit!*

The fifteenth chapter of John has much to say about fruit bearing. We are told that "every branch that beareth not fruit He taketh away: and every branch that beareth fruit, He purgeth it, that it may bring forth MORE fruit . . . He that abideth in me, and I in him, the same bringeth forth MUCH fruit . . . Herein is my Father glorified, that ye bear MUCH fruit . . . and that your fruit should remain." There is much in the New Testament concerning fruit bearing and the kind of fruit we bear.

In James 5:7 and 8 we read: "Be patient therefore, brethren, unto the coming of the Lord. Behold, the husbandman waiteth for the precious fruit of the earth, and hath long patience for it, until he receive the early and latter rain. Be ye also patient; stablish your hearts: for the coming of the Lord draweth nigh."

We are not to fret, we are to be patient. Jesus will come one day! Sometimes it may seem that He delays His coming, but we dare not suggest that God has made a mistake in allowing wickedness to advance and many times seemingly hinder the work of the Lord. It is not up to us to produce great things. We are called to be patient and bear fruit. If we are faithful in sowing the seed, God will take care of the fruit.

"But the fruit of the Spirit is love, joy, peace, longsuffering, gentleness, goodness, faith, meekness, temperance: against such there is no law" (Gal. 5:22, 23). To the glory of God, every believer should bear this fruit; it is the believer's fruitbasket.

"And the fruit of righteousness is sown in peace of them that make peace" (James 3:18). Jesus said, "Blessed are the peacemakers." Believers should bear fruit that produces peace—not hatred, animosity, strife, and division. A true Christian should live a life that will weld the Church together—not separate believers and cause dissension among them.

"But now being made free from sin, and become servants to God, ye have your fruit unto holiness, and the end everlasting life" (Rom. 6:22). Believers should bear the fruit of Bible holiness, and in so doing cause others to desire to know our Lord and Saviour, Jesus Christ.

"And that which fell among thorns are they, which, when they have heard, go forth, and are choked with cares and riches and pleasures of this life, and bring no fruit to perfection" (Luke 8:14). This verse describes the sad life of Many church people.

"Either make the tree good, and his fruit good; or else make the tree corrupt, and his fruit corrupt: for the tree is known by his fruit" (Matt. 12:33). We dare not judge our fellowman, but according to these words from the lips of Jesus, *by their fruits we shall know them*. If a person bears fruit of unrighteousness, ungodliness, and sin, we know that the heart is corrupt. It is from the heart that the issues of life proceed and the heart is responsible for the fruit one bears. If we name the name of Jesus, if we profess to be followers of the Son of God, we should bear the fruit described in Galatians 5:22. Believers are chosen, ordained, and commissioned to bear fruit.

10. *Believers Have a Glorious Privilege and a Grave Responsibility*:

It is a grand and glorious privilege to be a Christian. To be called a son of God is marvelous, wonderful, and certainly something for which to be thankful and praise God. On the assurance of God's Word we know that we have the seal of God upon our hearts; we know that we have access into the very presence of God through the blood of Jesus Christ. We know that our names are written in the Lamb's book of life and that we now possess divine nature.

We know that we have a great High Priest, the Lord Jesus Christ, who has entered into the presence of God with blood for us, and we know that He is ourAdvocate with the Father. We know that we have an unction—the anointing of the Holy Ghost. We know that we have a good conscience toward God, and that our heart condemns us not.

We know that we have the light of Jesus Christ—a lamp to our feet, a light unto our pathway. We have perfect confidence in the Lord Jesus Christ, and we possess the mind of Christ. Last, but by no means least, we know that we have been called and ordained of God to make disciples of men. In all of these things, we have a grand and glorious privilege that words cannot describe—*but so great the privilege, so weighty and grave the responsibility*.

If we profess to be followers of Jesus Christ, we must be an example of the believer. We must not stand in the way of sinners nor sit in the seat of the scornful. We must not live in such a way as to offend men and drive them from Christ. If we see the wicked in his way and fail to warn him, we are clearly taught that he will die in his sins and burn in hell, but his blood will be required at our hands (Ezek. 3:18, 20; 33:8, 9). It is a grave responsibility to be a Christian:

"We are the only Bible this careless world will read;
We are the sinner's Gospel, we are the scoffer's creed!"

Unbelievers may not read the Bible, but they will watch every move a Christian makes. That is why Jesus said, "Let your light so shine before men, that they may see your good works, and glorify your Father which is in heaven" (Matt. 5:16).

In closing, let me simply say, *Believers are saved, ordained, and commissioned to bear fruit.* Is your life fruitful? By bearing much fruit you glorify Jesus. How much fruit have borne for the Christ who died on the cross that you might be saved? God forgive us for bearing so little fruit, when our calling is from the One who gave ALL and who is *willing to give us all things*— whatsoever we will use to glorify His name and bring men unto Him. God help us to be fruit-bearing Christians!